Discrimination *in Society*

Religious Discrimination

Peggy J. Parks

ReferencePoint Press

San Diego, CA

About the Author
Peggy J. Parks is an author who has written dozens of educational books on a wide variety of topics for teens and young adults. She lives in Muskegon, Michigan, a town she says inspires her writing because of its location on the shores of beautiful Lake Michigan.

For more information, contact:
ReferencePoint Press, Inc.
PO Box 27779
San Diego, CA 92198
www.ReferencePointPress.com

Picture Credits:
Cover: Elenabsl/Shutterstock.com

5: Associated Press
12: Maury Aaseng
14: David McGlynn/Splash News
18: Rawpixel.com/Shutterstock.com
23: Ryan DeBerardinis/Shutterstock.com
26: Associated Press
30: Go Nakamura/ZUMA Press/Newscom
33: The Civil Rights Act of being enacted by
    President Lyndon Johnson, July 2, 1964./

Universal History Archive/UIG/Bridgeman
    Images
38: Associated Press
40: Daniel Karmann/picture-allience/dpa/AP
    Images
46: a katz/Shutterstock.com
48: Frances M. Roberts/Newscom
52: futurewalk/Shutterstock.com
56: Matt Goins/TNS/Newscom
61: Rick Wilking/Reuters/Newscom
65: Bob Brawdy/TNS/Newscom

LIBRARY OF CONGRESS CATALOGING-IN-PUBLICATION DATA

Name: Parks, Peggy J., 1951– author.
Title: Religious Discrimination/by Peggy J. Parks.
Description: San Diego, CA: ReferencePoint Press, [2019] | Series:
 Discrimination in Society | Audience: Grade 9 to 12. | Includes
 bibliographical references and index.
Identifiers: ISBN 9781682823880 (eBook) | ISBN 9781682823873
(hardback)
Subjects: LCSH: Religious discrimination in employment—Juvenile literature. |
 Law and legislation—Juvenile literature.

CONTENTS

The Ugliness of Bigotry

When someone disapproves of individuals or groups solely because of their religion, the person is said to be prejudiced or bigoted. Although not everyone acts on such feelings, bigotry is at the root of religious discrimination. Choosing not to live in the same neighborhood as Jewish families, refusing to rent an apartment or sell a home to Muslims, or telling a young man of the Sikh religion that he cannot wear his turban in school or at work are just a few examples of religious discrimination. It is possible for people of any faith to be discriminated against because of their religion, but research has shown that Jews and Muslims experience discrimination far more than people of other religions.

In the worst possible situations, religious discrimination leads to criminal activity, which is known as a religious hate crime. Hate crimes are serious, often deadly, crimes such as arson, vandalism, assault, rape, and murder. What makes them hate crimes is that they are committed because of religious hatred.

Religious Discrimination at Its Most Extreme

Twenty-five-year-old Marq Vincent Perez from Victoria, Texas, committed a hate crime in early 2017. Among his acquaintances, Perez was well-known for hating all people who practice the religion of Islam. On his Facebook page, he demeaned Muslims by referring to them as "rag heads" and "towel heads."[1] He was convinced that all Muslims were secretly members of the terrorist organization ISIS and therefore posed a threat to the United States. Perez believed it was his duty to rid his community of this perceived threat. So, he decided to burn down the mosque where local Muslims worshipped.

On January 28, 2017, Perez broke into the Victoria Islamic Center, disabled the alarm system, and set fire to the building with an explosive device. The blaze quickly took hold and soon was

The Victoria Islamic Center in Texas burns in January 2017. Investigators determined the cause to be arson. The perpetrator was also charged with damaging a religious property, which is a hate crime.

racing out of control. By the time police and firefighters arrived, the entire structure was engulfed in flames and beyond saving. "I just stood in the parking lot, feeling like my dream was being burned in front of my eyes,"[2] says Osama Hassan, the imam (worship leader) at the mosque. When the fire was finally extinguished, only two gold domes remained intact; the rest of the mosque was a total loss. An investigation found the cause of the fire to be arson. In June 2017 Perez was charged with arson and with damaging a religious property, which is a hate crime. If convicted, he could spend up to forty years in prison.

Religious Harassment

Hate crimes are the most extreme example of religious discrimination because they involve a violent crime. Although religious harassment does not involve criminal activity, it is another serious form of religious discrimination. People who are harassed because of their religion are often subjected to cruel, abusive behavior, such as bullying. This could involve making insulting remarks about someone's religious beliefs or practices, calling them offensive names, or harassing them via e-mails or text messages.

Journalist and author Linda K. Wertheimer, who is Jewish, recalls a painful incident that occurred when she was in high school. Her history teacher was reading from a textbook about the Holocaust, which was the systematic killing of millions of Jews in Europe by Adolf Hitler and his Nazi regime. As the teacher was reading, the boy sitting behind Wertheimer leaned forward and whispered "kike," which is an ethnic slur for a Jew. He then told her that his grandfather had been a member of the Ku Klux Klan (KKK), a hate group that advocates white supremacy and so-called religious purity. "I said nothing and stared forward, refusing to reveal just how much the slur stung," says Wertheimer. "My high school teacher did not hear anything, and I never told him."[3]

Religious harassment and other forms of religious discrimination are illegal. Federal law, for instance, protects people in all aspects of employment, from recruiting and interviewing to hiring, promotion, and termination. The US Department of Justice (DOJ) offers a scenario about a man of the Mormon faith who applies for a job. Although he meets the required qualifications, a supervisor opts not to hire him and is overheard telling a colleague that he would not feel comfortable working with a Mormon. In the process, the supervisor is breaking federal law.

Housing is another area where religious discrimination is known to occur, even though that is also illegal. If someone discriminates based on religion when selling or renting a home or apartment, it is a violation of federal law. But laws do not always prevent such behavior. One person who experienced this is Fatma Farghaly. In October 2016 she responded to a Craigslist ad for an apartment in Elizabeth, New Jersey. Because she is an observant Muslim, Farghaly was wearing a head covering known as a hijab. When the landlord first saw her, he asked if she was Muslim. She responded by saying yes, and he told her to leave because he did not rent to Muslims. Farghaly used her smartphone to record video of the incident, and she later filed a complaint with the state civil rights commission.

> "Even today, far too many people in this country face discrimination, harassment, and violence simply because of their religious beliefs."[4]
>
> —Vanita Gupta, the former head of the DOJ's Civil Rights Division

A Pressing Issue

Although it is widely known that religious discrimination occurs throughout the United States, the exact prevalence remains unknown. That is largely because there is no national system for tracking discrimination against people based on their religion. The only system designed to track discriminatory incidents is the FBI's tracking of hate crimes. According to its February 2018 report, nearly thirteen hundred religious hate crimes were reported by police departments throughout the United States during 2016. Experts say that the actual number is likely much higher because many people do not report discriminatory acts to the police, even when they meet the definition of hate crimes.

Despite the absence of exact prevalence figures, there is plenty of evidence that religious discrimination is a fact of life for people throughout the United States. Vanita Gupta, the former head of the DOJ's Civil Rights Division, writes,

> One of our nation's fundamental principles is that all people—regardless of where they worship or what they believe—are entitled to equal protection and fair treatment under the law. . . . Sadly, we have not always lived up to these lofty ideals. And even today, far too many people in this country face discrimination, harassment, and violence simply because of their religious beliefs.[4]

CHAPTER 1

How Serious a Problem Is Religious Discrimination?

Unlike some countries where people's rights to practice religion are severely restricted, freedom of religion is a guaranteed right in the United States. The First Amendment to the US Constitution states that "Congress shall make no law respecting an establishment of religion, or prohibiting the free exercise thereof."[5] With that one sentence, the Constitution declares that the government is not allowed to establish an official religion for the country, endorse one religion over another, or interfere with people's right to practice whatever religion they choose, including no religion. Numerous laws have also been enacted to further protect citizens' rights to be free from discrimination. Yet even with these legal protections, people throughout the United States continue to endure discrimination because of their religious beliefs—and the problem appears to be getting worse.

Most Discrimination Is Against Muslims

Research has shown that Muslims in America experience more discrimination than people of any other religious faith. One study that surveyed the prevalence of religious discrimination was conducted by the Institute for Social Policy and Understanding in 2017. More than twenty-three hundred Americans were asked to share their experiences (if any) with religious discrimination. When asked if they had personally experienced discrimination in the past year because of their religion, 60 percent of Muslims said they had. This was significantly higher than any other group surveyed, including Jews, of whom 38 percent said they had experienced religious discrimination. Among Christians, 8 percent of Catholics and 18 percent of Protestants said they had been discriminated against because of their religion.

The institute's survey also revealed that religious harassment is a serious problem among Muslims, including children attending school. In fact, Muslims were nearly twice as likely to report bullying of their school-age children as Jews, and they were four times as likely as the general public. When asked about bullying related to their religion, 42 percent of Muslim families said their children had experienced it at school. In a number of these cases, teachers or other school officials were involved in the bullying. This happened in Broward County, Florida, where two teachers were punished in 2017 for harassing Muslim students. One of the teachers, William Whalen, reportedly told a Muslim eighth grade boy, "We don't need another terrorist in this class."[6] He then pushed the boy out the door. The second teacher, Nancy Dean, taught high school. Like Whalen, she was accused of calling Muslim students terrorists.

Numerous religious harassment cases have also been reported among Muslim adults, such as a police officer in San Francisco, California. In April 2018 the officer (who chooses to remain anonymous) filed a complaint against the department, alleging he had been the target of religious harassment for the entire two years he has worked there. "I experienced blatant racism and bigotry toward me by some officers and sergeants," he says. According to the officer, some of his fellow cops and superiors repeatedly accused him of being a terrorist and subjected him to offensive jokes and ethnic slurs. One of them asked the officer if he knew any "towel heads," and another said that he supported a national travel ban that would keep Muslims out of the United States. The officer once went to his police station locker and found the words "ISIS go back" scrawled on the front. "I told them many times that their racist comments and actions towards me needed to stop," he says. "When their behavior escalated, that's when I decided to make a formal complaint." [7]

> "I experienced blatant racism and bigotry toward me by some officers and sergeants." [7]
>
> —A Muslim police officer from San Francisco

An Alarming Spike in Anti-Semitism

After Muslims, Jews are the most discriminated-against religious group in the United States, with 38 percent of them reporting discrimination. According to the Anti-Defamation League (ADL), an organization that fights anti-Semitism (hostility or prejudice against Jews), there has been a disturbing increase in anti-Semitic incidents in the United States. According to a February 2018 report by the ADL, between 2016 and 2017 such incidents jumped nearly 60 percent, which was the largest single-year increase on record.

Particularly worrisome is the increase in anti-Semitic incidents against children—a 94 percent spike from 2016 to 2017 among students in kindergarten through twelfth grade. In fact, elementary, middle, and high schools collectively had the highest number of anti-Semitic incidents over that period, surpassing public spaces, homes, workplaces, Jewish institutions, and college campuses. Even with these high numbers, experts say, the actual prevalence is likely much higher, as most of these incidents are not reported. "Enhanced reporting and heightened sensitivity to bullying has certainly contributed to the increase in reported incidents," says the ADL, "but the nature of schoolyard bullying makes it likely that these reported incidents are actually an underrepresentation of the total amount of anti-Semitic harassment against Jewish students." [8]

Anti-Semitic Incidents Soared in 2017

Religious discrimination is a problem throughout the United States, with the greatest number of incidents affecting Muslims and Jews. A 2018 report that documents religious discrimination against Jews, for instance, reveals a 60 percent spike in anti-Semitic incidents (including harassment, vandalism, and assault) between 2016 and 2017. This represents the largest single-year increase on record.

Anti-Semitic Incidents in the US Over the Last Decade

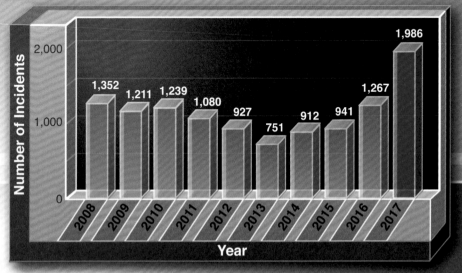

Source: Anti-Defamation League, "Anti-Semitic Incidents Surged Nearly 60% in 2017, According to New ADL Report," February 27, 2018. www.adl.org.

Most of these incidents involved harassment of Jewish students by their peers. There were also 221 instances of vandalism, such as Nazi swastikas drawn or scratched on school facilities, Jewish students' desks or notebooks, or their personal property. In December 2016, three swastikas were found on the grounds of an Orlando, Florida, high school. One had been painted on a rock, another on the pavement, and the third on a "no parking" sign. In January 2017 a Jewish student at a high school in Lexington, Kentucky, found a swastika that someone had drawn on the bathroom wall. The following month in Orlando, twelve-year-old Stella Cohen found three swastikas drawn on a seat in her school bus. "I don't know why somebody would be so rude," she says.

Cohen, who is Jewish, even wondered if she was somehow to blame for the incident. "Did I do something?"[9] she asks.

One state that has experienced a dramatic rise in anti-Semitic incidents is California, especially the northern part of the state. At schools in the San Francisco area, for instance, Jewish teens have found swastikas, references to Hitler, ethnic slurs, and other anti-Semitic references. Natasha Waldorf is one of those teens. She attends high school in Alameda and has experienced vicious anti-Semitic harassment. When Natasha was a freshman in 2016, she received anonymous text messages calling her a "kike." In another text someone told her that people hate Jews and that Hitler's biggest mistake was not killing her family during the Holocaust. There were other incidents as well. Once, when Natasha and a Jewish classmate were waiting for class to start, they heard two boys making jokes about the Holocaust. And scrawled on a desk in one of her classrooms, Natasha found the words, "JEWS ARE EVIL" along with swastikas and other anti-Semitic graffiti. "I wasn't sure if someone was out to get me or not," she says. "I just couldn't believe that someone could do something so cold-hearted."[10]

Bigotry Against Sikhs

People of the Sikh faith also report a frightening increase in religious discrimination and harassment. Sikhism, which originated in India, is the world's fifth-largest religion. It is part of the code of conduct for Sikhs to not cut their hair and to keep their heads covered. Male Sikhs typically have long beards and wear turbans, and females wear either turbans or headscarves. Along with keeping their own hair intact, Sikh parents are expected to follow the same practice with their children, including covering their heads and not cutting their hair. Although there may be a number of reasons why Sikhs are targeted for religious discrimination, many believe it is because they are often mistaken for Muslims. Others are convinced that it stems from widespread

Prabhjot Singh (far left) speaks to reporters about being attacked and beaten because of his Sikh faith and appearance. Singh, who is a physician, says bias-motivated attacks against Sikhs are increasing.

discrimination toward anyone who looks Middle Eastern. "It seems to make very little difference if the brown, bearded man with the turban calls himself a Sikh and not a Muslim," says Valarie Kaur, a Sikh civil rights advocate. "They read us as un-American."[11]

Physician and community health specialist Prabhjot Singh, who is Sikh, has observed an alarming rise in religious discrimination against people of his faith. He attributes this largely to an increase in anti-Muslim sentiment throughout the United States. According to Singh, the majority of Sikh students in America's public schools experience bullying and harassment because of their religion. "Some of our children are accused of being 'terrorists,'" says Singh. "Others have had their turbans ripped off."

Singh goes on to say that people of his religion are often called "ragheads" and "towelheads,"[12] and are accused of being part of the terrorist groups ISIS and al Qaeda. He has personally experienced this kind of bigotry, and it nearly cost him his life. In September 2013, as Singh was walking in New York City, a group of twenty or thirty young men knocked him down and began punching his face and body. He was badly injured in the brutal attack, including having his jaw broken. Singh is convinced that his injuries would have been much worse, perhaps even fatal, if bystanders had not intervened.

> "Some of our children are accused of being 'terrorists.' Others have had their turbans ripped off."[12]
>
> —Prabhjot Singh, a physician and community health specialist who practices Sikhism

Legislation

Such violent actions against people of a particular religion are often classified as hate crimes, and they are punishable under federal law. The first hate crime legislation was signed into law by President Lyndon B. Johnson in 1968. Since then it has been a federal crime to use (or threaten to use) force against someone because of his or her race, color, religion, sex, or national origin. States have also passed their own laws related to hate crimes. As of 2018, forty-five states and the District of Columbia had enacted hate crime legislation.

Throughout the years the federal government has passed other laws designed to address religious discrimination. People are protected at their workplace, for example, under Title VII of the federal Civil Rights Act of 1964. Under Title VII, employers are not allowed to discriminate against anyone based on race, color, religion, sex, or national origin. This covers every aspect of employment, from recruiting potential employees through advertising to hiring, fringe benefits, promotions, job assignments, training, and job termination. Title VII is enforced by a federal government agency known as the Equal Employment Opportunity Commission (EEOC).

Employers are also obligated to ensure that their employees are not harassed because of their religious beliefs—or their lack of religious beliefs. Religious harassment is considered a form of religious discrimination, which means it is prohibited under Title VII. The EEOC defines harassment as unwelcome conduct based on race, color, religion, sex, national origin, disability, or other factors. To be considered harassment, says employment lawyer Lisa Guerin, comments or actions must be severe enough, and pervasive enough, to alter the working environment. Occasional teasing or joking about an employee's religious beliefs, for instance, would not be an example of harassment. Guerin adds, however, that if "coworkers constantly joked and teased the employee about his faith, even after the employee made clear that he was uncomfortable and unhappy about it, that might be harassment."[13]

Legal Protection Outside the Workplace

Along with employment-related antidiscrimination laws, people are also protected in other ways, such as when they are searching for a place to live. The Fair Housing Act, which was signed into law in 1968, expanded on the Civil Rights Act of 1964. The Fair Housing Act prohibits anyone from refusing to rent or sell to people based on a number of factors, including their religion. The DOJ offers an example of this type of religious discrimination: "A Sikh man wearing a turban is told by a landlord that there are no apartments available in a complex, but later the same day the landlord tells other prospective tenants that there are units available."[14] If such an incident occurs—and research has shown that incidents like this do take place—the landlord is in violation of federal law.

Another antidiscrimination law, Title II of the Civil Rights Act of 1964, prohibits religious discrimination in public accommodations, which are facilities used by the public. This includes a wide variety of establishments, such as restaurants, hotels, cafés, the-

Bigotry and Hate Fueled by the Internet

Research has shown that religious discrimination is a serious problem that grows more serious as time goes by. Although no one can say with certainty what is causing this escalation of religious bigotry, civil rights advocates have theories about it. One of the most likely factors, according to the ADL's chief executive officer, Jonathan A. Greenblatt, is the Internet—especially social media—which he says has fueled the growth and spread of religious discrimination. "Anti-Semitism, Islamophobia, racism, and other hatreds have exploded online," says Greenblatt. He adds that the worldwide reach of the Internet, coupled with the soaring popularity of Twitter and other social media, has given those who harass, bully, and discriminate against people a much larger audience than ever before. "It provides instant and anonymous access to propaganda that can inspire and guide criminal activity," he says.

ADL research revealed that during 2017, millions of anti-Semitic messages on Twitter spread negative stereotypes and conspiracy theories about Jews. An estimated 3 million Twitter users either tweeted or retweeted at least 4.2 million anti-Semitic messages over a twelve-month period ending in January 2018. In addition, Twitter has proved to be a breeding ground for anti-Muslim sentiments, conspiracy theories, and false information about the religion of Islam.

Quoted in Homeland Security Digital Library, "Responses to the Increase in Religious Hate Crimes," Naval Postgraduate School, Center for Homeland Defense and Security, May 2, 2017. www.hsdl.org.

aters, parks, community centers, recreational facilities, museums, libraries, pharmacies, and retail stores. Under federal law, people of all religious faiths are free to patronize these and other establishments without interference related to their religion or religious practices.

Yet there are innumerable reports of that happening. One of these incidents occurred in May 2016 at a restaurant in Laguna Beach, California. Seven Muslim women were ordered to leave the restaurant, and they are convinced it was because they were wearing head scarves, or hijabs. Restaurant management disputed that, saying the women were asked to leave because the

A group of young Muslim women enjoy a meal together. A similar group of women say they were singled out because of their hijabs and asked by a restaurant employee to leave.

restaurant was very busy and they had exceeded the forty-five-minute time limit allowed for patrons to occupy a table. Video of the incident, however, showed tables throughout the restaurant that were empty. "I cried the whole way home," says Sara Farsakh, one of the women who was told to leave. "I was just so shocked and hurt by what happened."[15]

Tracking Religious Discrimination in Schools

Such discriminatory incidents have been reported throughout the United States, with a large number occurring at elementary and secondary schools. This is true even though federal and state laws are supposed to protect students from religious discrimination. Education officials have been unable to determine the severity of the problem on a national level because there was no tracking system in place. That changed in September 2016, when the US Department of Education launched a new tracking system.

For the first time ever, schools nationwide are required to report all incidents of religious-based bullying and harassment using an online data collection platform.

The expanded antidiscrimination effort includes a new website on religious discrimination, a complaint form that clarifies for schools the kinds of incidents that must be reported, a survey of public schools on religious-based bullying, legal information regarding students' religious rights, and a searchable database that parents can use if they are trying to locate the safest schools for their children to attend. "Students of all religions should feel safe, welcome and valued in our nation's schools," says attorney Catherine E. Lhamon, who is chair of the US Commission on

A Hurtful, Hateful Crime

In February 2017 an act of malicious vandalism was discovered in St. Louis, Missouri, at one of the oldest Jewish cemeteries in the state. Someone entered the cemetery and pushed over 170 headstones, breaking a dozen of them, including some that belonged to Jewish war veterans. This happened during the same period that bomb threats against Jewish community centers and other Jewish institutions were being phoned in throughout the United States. Because of that, many people were convinced that the act of vandalism was a religious hate crime against Jews. Families were devastated to learn that their relatives' graves had been violated.

In April 2017 police arrested the vandal: thirty-four-year old Alzado Harris, who was tracked down after police found a jacket he had left at the cemetery. Police could find no evidence of the crime being motivated by religious bias, so they charged him with institutional vandalism, not with a hate crime. Still, if convicted, Harris faces up to seven years in prison. "While it won't be prosecuted as a hate crime, there is no question that at the time it certainly felt hateful to the Jewish community, both in St. Louis and far beyond," says the ADL. Thanks to massive community support, including a fund-raising campaign by Muslim groups, all the headstones were either repaired or replaced, and Jews whose relatives were buried in the cemetery said they finally had a sense of closure.

Quoted in Anti-Defamation League, "ADL Welcomes Arrest in St. Louis Jewish Cemetery Desecration," April 25, 2018. http://stlouis.adl.org.

Civil Rights. "We will continue to work with schools and communities to stop discrimination and harassment so that all students have an equal opportunity to participate in school no matter who they are, where they come from or which faith, if any, they subscribe to."[16]

A Formidable Problem

More than two hundred years ago, America's founders established certain fundamental principles when they wrote and ratified the Constitution. One of these principles was religious freedom; that is, the freedom to worship without government interference. Since that time, religious liberty—including freedom from discrimination based on religion—has become central to the American way of life. "Religious liberty," says the DOJ, "is the 'first freedom' listed in the First Amendment of the Bill of Rights. A critical component of religious liberty is the right of people of all faiths to participate fully in the benefits and privileges of society without facing discrimination based on their religion."[17]

> "A critical component of religious liberty is the right of people of all faiths to participate fully in the benefits and privileges of society without facing discrimination based on their religion."[17]
>
> —US Department of Justice

Despite the importance US society places on religious freedom, discrimination based on religion still exists. In cities and towns throughout the United States, Jews, Muslims, Sikhs, and people of other religious faiths are still the targets of religious-based harassment and hate crimes. But growing public awareness and better enforcement of antidiscrimination laws might one day bring an end to this problem.

CHAPTER 2

Religious Hate Crimes

Hate crimes are not the same as other crimes. Whether they involve assault, vandalism of property, or threats of violence, hate crimes feel very personal to anyone who experiences them. "They strike at the heart of one's identity," says former FBI director James B. Comey. "They strike at our sense of self, our sense of belonging. The end result is loss: loss of trust, loss of dignity and, in the worst case, loss of life."[18]

A Worsening Problem

Each year in the United States, says the FBI, one hate crime is committed every ninety minutes. The FBI has been tracking and documenting hate crimes since shortly after legislation known as the Hate Crime Statistics Act became law in 1990. Reports of hate crime incidents are collected from federal, state, and local law enforcement officials throughout the country. The FBI's hate crime report of November 2017 shows that 6,121 hate crimes were committed in the United States during 2016. Of those, religious-related hate crimes were the second most-prevalent after racially motivated hate crimes.

Most religious hate crimes during 2016 were committed against Jews. One such crime occurred in October 2016. Eighteen-year-old Eric Carbonaro of Warwick, New York, maliciously defaced stone walls at the entrance of a Jewish cemetery. Using red spray paint, Carbonaro covered the walls in anti-Semitic graffiti, including swastikas, other Nazi symbols, and "Heil Hitler," a term that indicated obedience to Adolf Hitler during the Nazi regime. When confronted with the crime, Carbonaro admitted that it was motivated by his religious bias against Jews, and he pleaded guilty. "There is no room for this type of hateful desecration of religious property here in Orange County,"[19] says David Hoovler, who is district attorney for Orange County, New York.

The second highest incidence of hate crimes committed in 2016 targeted Muslims. Hate crimes against Muslims actually jumped 19 percent between 2015 and 2016. This was the biggest increase in religious hate crime since the terrorist attacks of September 11, 2001, known as 9/11. "Religious hate crimes against Muslims are the fastest growing category," says Charles Grassley, a US senator from Iowa who chairs the Senate Judiciary Committee. "Fear for practicing one's religion should never happen in this country. This problem has been growing for some time, and is not new."[20]

> "Fear for practicing one's religion should never happen in this country. This problem has been growing for some time, and is not new."[20]
>
> —Charles Grassley, a US senator from Iowa

One of these hate crimes occurred in New York City in December 2016. Aml Elsokary is a police officer and a Muslim. While off duty, she was parking the car while her teenage son waited for her. As she walked toward him on a Brooklyn street, she saw that a man was yelling at him and shoving him around. When she intervened to stop the man, he shouted "ISIS" at her, and he then started threatening her, saying, "I will cut your throat! Go back to your country!"[21] The man then fled. Within twenty-four hours police had him in custody and had charged him with felony aggravated harassment, elevated to a hate crime.

New York City, with its large and diverse population, reports the most hate crimes of any city in the United States. This is true even though overall crime in New York has plummeted over the years. Yet the FBI report shows that hate crimes in the city rose

Pedestrians and cars vie for space in New York City at rush hour. With its large and diverse population, New York City reports more hate crimes than any other US city.

12.4 percent during 2016, which was nearly triple the national increase. Of the total hate crimes committed in New York, says civil rights attorney Brian Levin, about 60 percent were motivated by religion as hate crimes against Jews and Muslims doubled in number. "Anti-Semitic & Anti-Muslim cases hit multi-year highs and account for over half of all NYC hate crime,"[22] says Levin. Other cities cited by the FBI for a high incidence of religious hate crimes in 2016 include Los Angeles; Phoenix, Arizona; and Washington, DC.

A Much Bigger Problem

Some experts believe that hate crimes are much more common than the FBI numbers show. According to the nonprofit investigative news organization ProPublica, a national crime victimization survey conducted by the federal Bureau of Justice Statistics shows the number of hate crimes to be closer to 250,000. That is a stark contrast to the FBI's reported 6,121 hate crimes. "The

Random Hatred

Research has shown that anti-Muslim bigotry is widespread in the United States. According to the FBI, hate crimes targeting Muslims increased 19 percent from 2015 to 2016. During this period, a number of religious hate crimes were committed against people of Middle Eastern descent who, because of their appearance and/or clothing, were assumed to be Muslim. This was the case with Hasel Afshar of Troutdale, Oregon. His home was vandalized—inside and out—in March 2017 while he was out of town for three days. Afshar, who immigrated to the United States from Iran in 2010, practices the Baha'i religion. But those who committed a hate crime against him obviously believed that he practiced Islam.

Virtually every surface of Afshar's home had been covered in hateful messages painted in huge letters. The words "Muslim," "kill you," "hate," and "die," shouted at him from the walls of every room, and "terrorist" was splashed across the kitchen cupboards and several walls in bright red paint. Also painted in red on cupboards and appliances was the threatening message, "Get out of America." In addition, furniture throughout the home was slashed, and the front door was hacked with a hatchet. Afshar was frightened as well as heartbroken that someone would hate him enough to destroy his home—solely because of perceived religious beliefs. "The irony here is almost painful," he says. "I left Iran to avoid being persecuted by Muslims, and now I'm being persecuted because someone thought I was Muslim."

Hasel Afshar, "I'm Baha'i, but I Was the Victim of an Anti-Muslim Hate Crime in America," *Islamic Monthly*, April 6, 2017. www.theislamicmonthly.com.

current statistics are a complete and utter joke,"[23] says Roy Austin, a prosecuting attorney who was formerly with the DOJ's Civil Rights Division.

Austin, along with the ADL and ProPublica, says that the reason for the FBI's underreporting of hate crimes is its reliance on local and state police departments to supply that data. Because doing so is voluntary, rather than mandatory, many law enforcement agencies either provide incomplete information or none at all. According to the ADL, more than ninety US cities with populations of at least 100,000 residents either reported zero hate crimes to the FBI during 2016 or ignored the agency's request for hate crime data altogether. In California, for instance, fewer than 30 percent of law enforcement agencies submitted hate crime data. In Massachusetts, fewer than 25 percent of the agencies submitted hate crime data. Hawaii submitted no hate crime data at all, and in Arkansas, Pennsylvania, and New Mexico just 1 percent of police departments submitted hate crime data. "There's a dangerous disconnect between the rising problem of hate crimes and the lack of credible data being reported," says Jonathan A. Greenblatt, the chief executive officer of the ADL. "Police departments that do not report credible data to the FBI risk sending the message that this is not a priority issue for them, which may threaten community trust in their ability and readiness to address hate violence."[24]

> "There's a dangerous disconnect between the rising problem of hate crimes and the lack of credible data being reported."[24]
>
> —Jonathan A. Greenblatt, the chief executive officer of the Anti-Defamation League

Another issue that compounds problems with compiling accurate hate crime statistics is the high number of federal law enforcement agencies that do not provide the FBI with that information. The FBI's Amy Blasher says federal law enforcement agencies are required to submit hate crime data to the FBI, but many do not. "We truly don't understand what's happening with crime in the US without the federal component,"[25] says Blasher. By neglecting to provide hate crime data to the FBI, these agencies are in violation of the law.

Disturbing Discoveries

The lack of accurate, comprehensive information on hate crimes motivated ProPublica to undertake a major project called Documenting Hate. Journalists spent a year documenting hate crimes of all types, including those that were motivated by religious bigotry. They tapped into a variety of sources, including social media, readers' personal accounts of hate crimes, and a coalition of more than 130 news media sources. They also interviewed law enforcement agencies throughout the United States, but those interviews yielded little information. As ProPublica journalist Ken Schwencke explains, "When we asked local law enforcement agencies across the country for their hate-crime reports and data, it quickly became clear that this was an area of substantial uncertainty and discomfort for many of them."[26]

During their yearlong investigation of hate crimes, ProPublica journalists learned a great deal, and much of what they discov-

Vandals have painted swastikas and other symbols of religious and ethnic hatred on the walls and steps of a Jewish synagogue in Maine. Police officers who are not trained to recognize hate crimes might classify this as simple vandalism.

ered was jarring. The investigation revealed, for instance, that more than half of hate crime victims never file reports with the police. And when hate crimes are reported, police are often not trained to handle them; thus, they do not write reports that specify hate crimes. One example is the Miami-Dade Police Department in Florida, the state's largest law enforcement agency, which has reported just two hate crimes since 2010. Argemis Colome, a detective and spokesman for Miami-Dade, shares his experience: "I was on the road for 9 years, but when I wrote a report, I don't ever remember titling it a hate crime. If they would have done graffiti on a wall, it would have been titled a vandalism."[27]

Even when police departments do report hate crime data, these crimes are rarely prosecuted. In Texas, for example, ProPublica found that 981 hate crimes were reported to police between 2010 and 2015, and only eight of those ended in convictions. The same is true in a number of other states. This happens for several reasons, including the challenge of proving that the act was motivated by religious, racial, or some other form of bias and hatred. "It's notoriously difficult," says Benjamin Wagner, the former US attorney for California's Eastern District. "You need to prove not just the incident, but the state of mind of the defendant—that what they intended was hate-motivated. That's never easy and often involves not just looking at the incident, but going back and investigating the background of the defendant."[28]

A Resurgence of Bigotry

During the course of the ProPublica investigation, journalists made some alarming discoveries about hate crimes. One of these discoveries was the widespread prevalence of bigotry and hatred toward Muslims throughout the United States. "Islamophobia remains a fact of life across America,"[29] says ProPublica journalist Rachel Glickhouse. Bigotry directed at Muslims soared in the aftermath of the 9/11 terrorist attacks, which were carried out by Islamist extremists.

Anti-Muslim sentiment is still disturbingly common in the United States. And it has had a spillover effect. The hatred that fuels crimes against Muslims has also affected people of other faiths and backgrounds. Non-Muslims who look Middle Eastern, or wear clothing or head coverings that are perceived to be Muslim, are as likely to be the target of a religious hate crime as someone who is actually Muslim. Eric Treene, a civil rights attorney with the DOJ, explains, "If someone is angry at Muslims, they will attack Sikhs, Middle-Easterners—people who look different."[30]

Physician and community health specialist Prabhjot Singh, who is a leader in the Sikh community, has grown increasingly troubled by what he views as a toxic political climate in the United States. In May 2017 Singh testified during a US Senate hearing titled, "Responses to the Increase in Religious Hate Crimes." He expressed concern about the level of hostility coming from the nation's political leaders. "I was horrified to hear our President last weekend telling thousands of people at a rally that immigrants are snakes waiting to bite America," Singh said. "Words matter, and when political leaders divide and dehumanize us, this lays the groundwork for hate to infect our society." He emphasized how the thoughtless words of political leaders can play a role in inciting hatred against Muslims. "I am particularly concerned about the staggering rise in anti-Muslim hate violence and anti-immigrant rhetoric, which increasingly appears to be tolerated—even celebrated—in our political discourse,"[31] said Singh. He went on to describe an alarming spike in hate crimes against people of his religion, often because people caught up in anti-Muslim furor hate all Middle Eastern religions.

One Sikh man who was the victim of a brutal hate crime in September 2016 is Maan Singh Khalsa. He was driving home from work in Richmond, California, when some clearly intoxicated men in a pickup truck pulled up next to him at a traffic light. They began cursing at him and threw a half-full can of beer at his car. When the light changed, Khalsa drove away and called 911 on his cell phone to report the incident. The truck followed him. When he

The Desire to Kill

Anti-Semitism is a serious and growing problem in the United States, and this has led to numerous hate crimes. According to data from the FBI, Jews are targeted in hate crimes more than any other religious group. In April 2018 police in Irvine, California, arrested a man on felony hate crime charges because of what detectives found when they searched his home. The man, twenty-six-year-old Nicholas Rose, had told relatives about his desire to kill Jews, and they contacted police.

The search of Rose's home yielded so-called kill lists that contained the names of community leaders and prominent Jews in show business. Detectives also found anti-Semitic literature as well as a distressing step-by-step guide that Rose had titled "Killing my first Jew." He was also apparently planning some kind of violence against a local synagogue and two churches that he disliked because of their friendliness toward Jews. When Rose's neighbor learned about his intentions, she was shocked. "It's really scary to think that there's someone with that kind of hate in their heart—planning stuff against Jewish people," she says.

Quoted in CBS Los Angeles, "Irvine Man Charged with Anti-Semitic Hate Crimes After Being Turned in by Family Member," April 19, 2018. http://losangeles.cbslocal.com.

stopped at another light, the truck pulled up next to him and three men got out and ran over to his car. One of them yanked Khalsa's head out of the open window and began punching him in the face, fracturing his eye socket. Another pulled Khalsa's turban off and, using a pocketknife, cut off about 10 inches (25 cm) of his hair. When Khalsa tried to shield his face from the attackers, one of his fingers was cut so severely with the knife that it had to be amputated.

The men were caught and charged with felony assault, which was elevated to a religious hate crime. "It will take me many years, maybe the rest of my life, to heal from this attack," says Khalsa. "But the recognition of the attack as a hate crime—as harm to my dignity and my entire community—is the first step in the process."[32]

Hate Crimes Versus Hate Speech

What happened to Khalsa was a hate crime: felony assault that was motivated by religious hatred. Many people are also under the impression that hateful speech falls under the category of hate crime, but that is often not the case. In the United States, free speech is guaranteed under the First Amendment, just as freedom of religion is. The only circumstances in which speech is illegal is if it incites individuals or groups to illegal activity, is directly related to a violent act, constitutes a threat that causes someone to fear violence, or rises to the level of harassment. "Hate itself is not a crime,"[33] says the FBI.

As a university law professor who has taught First Amendment law for more than three decades, Erwin Chemerinsky often answers tough questions about hate speech, including whether it should be illegal. While he understands people's reasoning for

Members of a white supremacist group march in Georgia in 2018. Hateful speech from groups like this may feel like a hate crime, but it is usually considered protected speech under the US Constitution.

wanting to outlaw hate speech, he believes that should not happen. One reason is because the Constitution does not allow it; even hateful speech is protected by the First Amendment. "Every effort by the government to regulate hate speech has been declared unconstitutional,"[34] says Chemerinsky.

Not everyone thinks that is how it should be. Law professor Liaquat Ali Khan believes that hate speech creates an atmosphere in which bias-related violence might seem acceptable to some people. Khan distinguishes between provocateurs, or those who use hate speech but rarely commit hate crimes, and perpetrators, who actually commit hate crimes. "I maintain that the provocateurs of hatred are much more dangerous than the perpetrators of hate crimes," he says. These are the people who spread religious hatred and "lay the foundation for violence." By maligning Islam, says Khan, "the provocateurs generate hatred not only against Muslims but also against Jews, Catholics, Mormons, Sikhs, and Hindus." He is convinced that such hate speech must be limited. "Without censoring free speech, the law has the tools to hold the provocateurs of hatred accountable," says Khan. "The whole world, except the United States, punishes the provocateurs of hate speech."[35]

> "No person should have to fear being violently attacked because of who they are, what they believe, of how they worship."[36]
>
> —US attorney general Jeff Sessions

A Bleak Outlook

Religious-based hate crimes are vicious, demoralizing, and terrifying. "No person should have to fear being violently attacked because of who they are, what they believe, of how they worship,"[36] says US attorney general Jeff Sessions. Data on hate crimes are often sketchy and incomplete, largely because so many are never reported. But because of the work of journalists and advocacy organizations like the ADL and others, it is starting to become clear that religiously motivated hate crimes are a serious and growing threat in the United States.

CHAPTER 3

Religious Discrimination in the Workplace

When the Civil Rights Act became law in 1964, it was hailed as one of the most important pieces of legislation in US history. It addressed different types of discrimination and devoted an entire section (Title VII) to discrimination in the workplace. Title VII applies to employers with fifteen or more workers, including government agencies (federal, state, and local) and private and public colleges and universities. The law prohibits these entities from discriminating based on race, color, religion, sex, or national origin. This covers all aspects of employment, from job recruitment and advertising to hiring, pay, benefits, job assignments, promotions, and termination.

Title VII broadly defines the word *religion*. It refers not only to traditional organized and recognized religions, such as Christianity, Judaism, Islam, Hinduism, and Buddhism, but also, says the EEOC, to "religious beliefs that are new, uncommon, not part of a formal church or sect, only subscribed to by a small number of people, or that seem illogical or unreasonable to others."[37] In addition to various forms of religion, Title VII protects workers from being discriminated against for having no religious beliefs.

The Prevalence of Workplace Discrimination

The Title VII prohibitions on workplace discrimination are clear, and those who violate the law risk substantial financial penalties. "The risks of getting it wrong—and, we believe, the rewards of getting it right—are powerful motivators to businesses to pay careful attention to this issue,"[38] says the ADL. One company that was hit with a large financial penalty for workplace discrimination was Kasco, which is based in St. Louis, Missouri, and sells butcher supplies and meat-processing equipment. Former employee Latifa Sidiqi reported that she was discriminated against after she started wearing a hijab to work and fasted during the Muslim holiday of Ramadan. When she complained about the discrimination, she was fired; she then sought the help of the EEOC. In April 2017, Kasco was found guilty and ordered to pay Sidiqi $110,000.

Yet even though Title VII has been in effect for more than fifty years, workplace-related religious discrimination continues to be reported throughout the United States. "Religious discrimination in the workplace is an issue that continues to fester in the US,"[39]

Members of Congress and other dignitaries watch as President Lyndon B. Johnson signs the Civil Rights Act of 1964. Title VII of the Civil Rights Act prohibits workplace discrimination based on race, color, religion, sex, and national origin.

says James Sonne, the founding director of Stanford Law School's Religious Liberty Clinic. During 2017 a total of 3,436 religion-related workplace discrimination claims were filed with the EEOC. Researchers say the amount has more than doubled since the 1990s.

According to Jason A. Cantone of the Federal Judicial Center in Washington, DC, and Richard L. Wiener of the University of Nebraska College of Law, the actual number of religion-based discrimination charges is significantly higher than what is reported to the EEOC. They write, "These rising numbers likely still underestimate the prevalence of religious discrimination in the workplace as much goes unreported when victims either do not feel their experience justifies a claim, fear retaliation, or unsuccessfully navigate the complex complaint process."[40]

Cantone and Wiener's study, which was published in July 2017, was one of the rare studies that focused exclusively on religious discrimination (rather than racial or sex discrimination) in the workplace. They found that more than one-third of American workers have experienced religious bias at work. Among non-Christian workers (mostly Jews and Muslims) the number is even higher: 56 percent. Because there is so much disparity in the collection of data about religion-related workplace discrimination, Cantone and Wiener emphasize the need for further study. "With the number of filed religious discrimination claims near record levels, additional research is timely and needed."[41]

Prevalence Expected to Grow

Some experts believe that workplace-related religious discrimination claims will continue climbing in the coming years. One explanation for this is the growing awareness of individual rights and a willingness to speak up when inappropriate events occur. Increased flexibility in the workplace might play a role in the growth of workplace discrimination claims too. According to attorney Jonathan A. Segal, the more flexible employers are with their workers, the more flexible they will need to be with employees with religious-related requests. "For example," he says, "how could you show that you can accommodate an employee leaving work early to pick up his son, but not to attend church?"[42]

Attorneys Barbara Hoey and Alyssa Smilowitz, who work for a labor and employment law firm in New York City, point out another factor contributing to increased workplace discrimination cases: new variations in religions that employers are expected to accommodate. A federal judge in New York, for example, ruled in

When Workplace Bullies Are Kids

When religious harassment occurs at someone's job, the harassers may be coworkers, supervisors, or even customers. For Maimona Afzal Berta, who teaches eighth grade in San Jose, California, the harassers were middle school students. Berta is Muslim and wears a hijab every day, including to the school where she teaches. She has reported numerous instances of religious harassment at school, including students making derogatory comments about her religion, Islam. They have yelled at her, accused her of being a terrorist, and kicked her classroom door while yelling "shoot her!" One day Berta arrived at school to find that her classroom windows and door had been covered with anti-Muslim slurs and obscenities. "It was devastating," she says. "I felt completely targeted and not even safe in a place I consider home."

Berta has reported the harassment to school officials many times. She says that even though they express sympathy toward her and anger over what has happened, they do not address the incidents in a timely manner. Also, says Berta, when students are caught, their punishment is far more lenient than she believes it should be. "You can't keep telling people that you care and want to stop hate, and yet you don't follow through with action," she says. Despite Berta's frustration with the school's handling of the harassment, when offered a transfer to a different school, she turned it down. "That's not solving the problem," she says. "I feel personally responsible so that this doesn't happen to anyone else."

Quoted in Sharon Naguchi, "Anti-Muslim Bullying by Pupils Targets Hijab-Wearing Teachers," *Mercury News*, November 24, 2017. www.mercurynews.com.

2016 that a belief system called Onionhead satisfied the test for a religion under Title VII. Onionhead is affiliated with the nonprofit group Harnessing Happiness, whose focus is infusing happiness and hope into everyday life. Hoey and Smilowitz write, "The court compared Onionhead to the 12-step Alcoholics Anonymous program, which the Second Circuit had previously found to be a religion under the law."[43]

Reasonable Accommodation

Under Title VII, employers are expected to make reasonable accommodations for the religious beliefs and practices of job candidates and employees. Some common examples of religious accommodations include flexible scheduling, voluntary shift substitutions or swaps, job reassignments, lateral transfers, modifications to workplace policies or practices, and exceptions to dress or grooming rules. An employee whose religion observes the Sabbath on a Saturday, for example, might request to switch shifts with a coworker to avoid working on a Saturday. If this causes the employer no problems, the employee's request must be accommodated. This requirement is only waived if an accommodation would cause the employer serious problems. "If it would not pose an undue hardship," says the EEOC, "the employer must grant the accommodation."[44]

Many companies go out of their way to accommodate their employees' religious practices and special needs. One of these is the accounting firm EY (formerly Ernst & Young), which has created quiet rooms at its New York City headquarters. Employees can use these rooms to reflect, pray, meditate, or just take a break from the busy work environment. EY also includes major religious and cultural holidays on its calendar to help with development of work schedules.

Not all employers make such efforts, and a large number of lawsuits reflect this. One example is a 2017 case involving a clerk at a Raley's supermarket in Chico, California. The clerk, Jennifer

Webb, is a Jehovah's Witness. At the time of her hiring, Webb explained that she could not work shifts after 5:00 pm on Wednesdays and before 4:00 pm on Sundays since those were times she attended religious meetings. When she was required to work late on a Wednesday before Thanksgiving, she said she was unable to do so and was fired. In September 2017 the EEOC filed a religious discrimination lawsuit on Webb's behalf. The company denied the claim and vowed to fight it.

Religious Clothing

In addition to work schedules, religious accommodation pertains to clothing people wear as part of their religious beliefs. Examples include a Jewish male who wears a brimless cap known as a *kippah* or a Muslim female who wears a hijab. For Hadas Goldfarb, a paramedic who lives in Brooklyn, the requested clothing accommodation was to wear a skirt while she worked rather than the customary pants. Goldfarb is an Orthodox Jew, and her religion's modesty tenet calls for women to wear skirts rather than pants.

In 2015 Goldfarb was hired by New York Presbyterian Hospital to work with its paramedic corps. She attended an orientation event where she received an employee manual that discussed acceptable attire and stated that skirts were forbidden. She explained to Michael Koppel, the hospital's director of paramedic services, that she wore skirts for religious reasons, and she requested that she be allowed to do so. Citing safety issues, Koppel said Goldfarb needed to comply with the standard dress code. When she objected, she was fired.

Goldfarb was shocked to lose her job. She had previously worked as a paramedic in Cleveland, Ohio, and wearing a skirt had never created any difficulties. "I've been an EMS for a while and I haven't had a problem—I just wasn't expecting it to be an issue,"[45] she says. In 2017 Goldfarb sued the hospital for failing to provide her with reasonable accommodation for her religious observance.

Religious clothing was also the reason for Samantha Elauf's lawsuit, and her case went all the way to the US Supreme Court. Elauf, who is Muslim, applied for a job at an Abercrombie Kids store in 2008 when she was seventeen years old. When she went to the interview, she was wearing her hijab, as she always did whenever she went out. Even though she was qualified, she did not get the job. She later learned that her hijab did not comply with the company's dress code, in which caps or any type of head coverings are forbidden.

When Elauf learned why she was not offered a position, she sought the EEOC's assistance; the agency filed a lawsuit on her behalf in 2009. After six years of court decisions and appeals, the Supreme Court ruled in Elauf's favor in 2015, emphasizing that employers are expected to make an effort to accommodate people's religious needs. By refusing to hire Elauf because of her religious garment, Abercrombie Kids was in violation of Title VII. When the ruling was announced, Elauf said she was grateful to the Supreme Court justices. "I was a teenager who loved fashion and was ea-

Samantha Elauf (right) and her mother stand outside the US Supreme Court, which ruled in her favor in 2015. Elauf was rejected for a job at Abercrombie Kids because her head scarf conflicted with the company's dress code.

ger to work for Abercrombie & Fitch," she says. "Observance of my faith should not have prevented me from getting a job. I am glad that I stood up for my rights, and happy that EEOC was there for me and took my complaint to the courts."[46]

An Unusual Accommodation

Under Title VII legislation, employers are obligated to do everything possible to accommodate their employees' religious beliefs and needs. Only if a request causes undue hardship for employers can they legally refuse to accommodate it. In the case of Beverly Butcher, a coal miner from West Virginia, the request was denied—and the employer ended up paying a high price for that. Butcher had worked for a mine in Mannington, West Virginia, for nearly forty years. During the summer of 2012 Consol Energy, the owner of the mine, installed a biometric hand scanner to better monitor employee attendance and work hours. Upon arrival at work and leaving at the end of a shift, each employee's right hand was scanned. The shape of the hand was then linked to his or her personnel number. Butcher, a devout evangelical Christian, wanted no part of the hand scanner. Based on the Bible's reference to the Mark of the Beast (leading to eternal separation from God), he feared that the scanner would mark his hand in a way that would doom him to eternal punishment. He asked to be excused from using the scanner because of his religious beliefs.

Consol refused Butcher's request, saying that the scanner would not mark his hand in any way. At the same time, two employees with hand injuries were allowed to enter their personnel numbers on a keypad instead of using the scanner, but Butcher was not offered the same accommodation. So, he retired from his job under protest and sought the assistance of the EEOC, who sued Consol on Butcher's behalf. After several court decisions

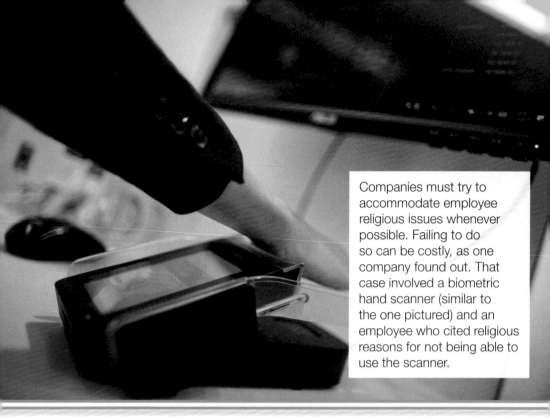

Companies must try to accommodate employee religious issues whenever possible. Failing to do so can be costly, as one company found out. That case involved a biometric hand scanner (similar to the one pictured) and an employee who cited religious reasons for not being able to use the scanner.

and appeals, Butcher was awarded nearly $600,000 in damages and lost benefits in June 2017. "As noted by the court," says attorney J. William Manuel, "an employer cannot escape the requirement to accommodate simply because they think the belief is stupid or mistaken. If there is enough evidence to show that the employee really believes it, you need to start looking at whether you can find some sort of accommodation."[47]

Workplace Harassment

Because harassment is a type of religious discrimination, it is also forbidden in the workplace under Title VII. Harassers might include supervisors, coworkers, or nonemployees, such as a vendor or customer. Many different actions could be considered harassment: offensive remarks (verbally or via e-mail or text) about a person's religion (including religious practices and clothing), slurs and name-calling, displaying offensive objects or pictures, and physical threats or assaults. The EEOC divides workplace harassment into two distinct types: quid pro quo ("this for that") harassment and hostile work environment harassment.

Quid pro quo harassment involves a situation in which an employee is required or pressured to abandon, change, or adopt religious beliefs as a condition of employment, to secure a promotion or raise in pay, or to avoid discipline or firing.

> "As noted by the court, an employer cannot escape the requirement to accommodate simply because they think the belief is stupid or mistaken."[47]
>
> —Employment attorney J. William Manuel

Lisa Guerin, an attorney who specializes in employment issues, offers the hypothetical example of an employee who is told that if she wants a promotion, she must attend a monthly meeting to study the principles of the Church of Scientology. Guerin offers another hypothetical example: a supervisor who is a devout Catholic and wants his employee to attend mass with him before work. The employee was raised Catholic but is no longer religious and declines the supervisor's request. The supervisor responds by telling the employee that he had been considering her for a major new project. If she had no interest in attending mass, however, she probably was not cut out for the project he had in mind. Because the employee's job was tied to attending mass, the EEOC would consider it quid pro quo harassment.

Hostile work environment harassment occurs when an employee is subjected to unwelcome conduct based on his or her religion. The conduct must be so severe or pervasive that it alters the terms and conditions of employment. It is also considered hostile work environment harassment when an employer tries to coerce employees into practicing a particular religion. This happened at United Health Programs of America, which had implemented the Harnessing Happiness (or Onionhead) belief system at their company—a decision that cost them $5.1 million.

According to employees who filed a lawsuit in 2014, United Health required them to partake in Harnessing Happiness activities starting in 2007. These activities involved saying prayers, participating in religious workshops, reading spiritual texts, saying

No Preaching Allowed

Under federal law, employers are obligated to maintain a work environment that is free from religious harassment, which includes refraining from forcing their own religious beliefs on employees. In 2013 Tyler Stille, a grocery store owner in Des Moines, Iowa, was cited by a state judge for this type of harassment. Afterward, Stille was dumbfounded by the ruling. He is a devout Christian and says everyone who knows him is aware of that, including his customers and employees. "We have a Christian fish symbol on our sign," says Stille. "Before we hire anybody, we tell them our faith. We play Christian music in our store all the time, and we always make sure that's OK with them because that's a part of our life."

The employee who filed the claim against Stille was Sherri Chafin, who worked for him from September 2011 to January 2012. She acknowledges knowing about his religious faith and says it never bothered her until she believes Stille went too far. According to Chafin, he began lecturing her, telling her she should read one verse from the Bible every day, and criticizing her lifestyle. After a confrontation in January 2012, Chafin left the store and never returned. She filed a claim against him, and in November 2013 a judge chastised Stille for his conduct toward Chafin, saying he had created an intolerable work environment with his preaching. He was also ordered to pay Chafin's unemployment benefits.

Quoted in Clark Kauffman, "Judge: Workplace Lecture Was Religious Harassment," *USA Today*, November 13, 2013. www.usatoday.com.

"I love you" to each other and to managers, and thanking God for their jobs. If they refused, they risked being fired, as Francine Pennisi was in August 2010. "If you weren't a follower of . . . Onionhead, you would be fired,"[48] she says, adding that the workplace atmosphere and required rituals were like a cult.

In April 2018, following a three-week trial, a jury in Brooklyn, New York, found that United Health (and its parent company, the Cost Containment Group, or CCG) had violated Title VII by forcing its employees to engage in religious activities. The company was ordered to pay $5.1 million in damages to Pennisi and the other employees who filed the lawsuit. "This case featured a unique type of religious discrimination," says EEOC trial attorney Charles Coleman Jr., "in that the employer was pushing its religion on employees. Nonetheless, Title VII prohibits religious discrimination of this sort and makes what happened at CCG unlawful. Employees cannot be forced to participate in religious activities by their employer."[49]

Trouble in the Workplace

The law about employment-related religious discrimination has been in place since 1964, and its requirements are quite clear: employers need to do everything possible to respect and accommodate their workers' religious beliefs and practices, unless such accommodation leads to problems. Those who do not make such an effort are subject to expensive lawsuits and stiff penalties if courts rule against them. Although many employers go out of their way to comply with the law, thousands of cases filed each year with the EEOC make it clear that the prevalence of workplace discrimination is high. And according to employment law specialists, the real number of cases is much higher than anyone knows.

CHAPTER 4

How People Are Hurt by Religious Discrimination

When people who experience religious discrimination are asked how it made them feel, they describe a range of emotions, from shock and humiliation to a sense of deep sadness. If they are harassed by someone who clearly hates them for what they believe, this can be terribly frightening and even make people fear for their lives. In May 2018 five young Muslim men in St. Augustine, Florida, felt that kind of fear—and had no idea if they would survive the threat they were facing.

The young men, all international students from Egypt, were standing by their cars outside a McDonald's restaurant. It was very late, about 1:30 a.m., and as they stood around talking and eating their burgers and fries, they noticed a man in a pickup truck watching them closely. Then he spoke to them. "Are you American boys?" he asked. Sensing that there could be trouble, the students did not respond to him, nor did they even look at him. Suddenly he started toward them with a pocket knife in his hand, flicking it open and closed, while shouting, "Get out of my country. You do not deserve to eat here."[50] At that moment, the five young men feared that they were about to die.

Fear Takes an Emotional Toll

One of the students used his cell phone to call the police, and officers arrived at the scene. They found the man, John Jay Smith, intoxicated and arrested him. One of the students, twenty-three-year-old Omar Abdelmoaty, said he and the others had been in the United States for months and had never experienced anything so frightening. When asked why they thought Smith had targeted them, Abdelmoaty had no doubt it was

because they are Muslims. This sort of hatred was very difficult for him and his friends to understand. "This is the land of the free, so we didn't think one day that we would encounter something like this," he says. "We didn't do anything to anybody. We're just students. The basic idea that he charged us and attacked us for this, for our religion, for our home country and background, it's kind of scary." Since the attack, all three young men have had difficulty sleeping at night, says Abdelmoaty. They have tried to get back to their normal routine, but the incident frightened them so badly it became difficult to even go out in public. "We're in a state of fear,"[51] he says.

Muslims throughout the United States feel afraid, according to a 2017 report by the Institute for Social Policy and Understanding (ISPU). Although this has been the case on and off since the 9/11 terrorist attacks, fears among Muslims have heightened since the 2016 presidential campaign and election. Threats against Muslims began to soar during the campaign, as candidate Donald Trump made numerous disparaging remarks about immigrants, including those who practice Islam. He made clear his intention to implement a ban on Muslims who want to come to the United States as a way of preventing terrorism. "Our country cannot be the victims of horrendous attacks by people that believe only in jihad and have no sense of reason or respect for human life,"[52] Trump said during a December 2015 speech in South Carolina. In many speeches he spoke about the need to severely restrict immigration and ban visitors from seven countries that are largely Muslim: Iraq, Syria, Iran, Sudan, Libya, Somalia, and Yemen. Trump also expressed support for heavy surveillance of mosques and said he would consider the creation of a nationwide database to track all Muslims in the country.

During and after the presidential campaign, Donald Trump made numerous disparaging remarks about Muslims. American Muslims fear these comments will lead to increased discrimination and physical attacks.

In January 2017 the ISPU surveyed more than twenty-three hundred Americans. The survey found that since the November 2016 election, 38 percent of Muslims and 27 percent of Jews feared for their personal safety (or their family's safety) from hate groups. Many Muslims and Jews also reported that they suffered emotionally with stress and anxiety more than they ever had before.

The Family Youth Institute, which is dedicated to the long-term mental health and well-being of American Muslims, reports seeing a sharp increase in cases of anxiety and depression since 2016. Muslims in the United States have been in "perpetual crisis mode"[53] in recent years, according to psychologist Rania Awaad, who is the director of a Muslim counseling center in San Francisco. Awaad says that after the 2016 presidential election, the center offered a support group for young Muslims who were afraid and in need of talking about what they were feeling. But when their parents arrived to drop them off, they would not leave—they wanted help too.

Scared Kids

All of the rhetoric about the so-called Muslim ban has added to the fears experienced by young Muslims in the United States. As promised during his campaign, Trump instituted the ban by executive order once he became president. Although three federal judges struck down the ban, the US Supreme Court allowed it to take effect in December 2017. The justices then heard arguments in the case in April 2018. A ruling was expected in June. Whatever the outcome, even if the ban were declared unconstitutional, it does not lessen the knowledge that the person who holds the highest office in the country has made some remarks that make young Muslims feel unwelcome, afraid, and insecure.

Even before the 2016 presidential election, teachers throughout the United States began observing a rise in fear and, in some instances, hysteria among Muslim children. One New York City school district administrator spoke with reporters about frightened, crying children at her schools. "Kids were sobbing, especially immigrant children, saying they were going to get sent back to Guinea, Senegal, Yemen," she says. "They were totally distraught. And then one kid would try to explain to another kid about deportation and it would turn into an argument about, 'You're going to get deported.' 'No, you are.'"[54]

The administrator recalls one sixth grader who was inconsolable. Teachers found him sobbing uncontrollably in a hallway one day between classes. When they asked him what was wrong, he said he had received detention. This had happened before, so at first the teachers wondered why he would be so upset. The boy explained that he and his family were from Senegal, a country in West Africa where 90 percent of the population is Muslim. He had heard about Trump's intention to ban Muslims from certain countries, and he assumed that Senegal was one of them. He thought that because he had gotten into trouble at school, he would be taken away from his family and sent back to Senegal. Even though Senegal was not one of the countries included in Trump's initial proposal for a Muslim ban, this was of little comfort

"Some Muslim students think that, if Trump becomes president, they will have microchips implanted under their skin."[55]

—Maureen B. Costello of the Southern Poverty Law Center

to a child who was scared and uncertain about his future.

During March and April 2016, the Southern Poverty Law Center (SPLC) gathered feedback from educators across the United States. Collectively, they provided more than five thousand comments. More than two-thirds of teachers reported that young people in their schools (most often immigrants from various countries, children of immigrants, Muslims, and children of color) had expressed concern about what might happen to them as a result of the presidential election. "Fears are pervasive," Maureen B. Costello of the SPLC said of the educators' feedback. "Students tell teachers they are worried about deportation, having their families split, being put in jail or attacked by police, losing their homes, seeing their places of worship closed, going into hiding and being sent to detention camps. Some Muslim students think that, if Trump becomes president, they will have microchips implanted under their skin."[55]

Immigrants from the mostly Muslim nation of Senegal walk and shop in New York. Educators nationwide have reported Muslim children feeling frightened about being sent away because of their faith. One such report concerned a child from Senegal.

Many of the comments shared by teachers were what they overheard students saying to each other. At a school in Helena, Montana, for instance, one teacher overheard a fifth grader telling a Muslim student that he supported Trump because he was going to "kill all of the Muslims."[56]

Bigotry Hurts

People of all ages can be hurt by religious discrimination, but it can be especially tough on kids. Children lack the ability to understand why anyone would dislike them just because of their religion, let alone hate them for it. They hear adults making bigoted, hate-filled remarks, and they also hear the same thing from classmates who repeat what the adults say. This can be extraordinarily confusing and hurtful for children. "Young children can't understand why people hate them without even knowing them,"[57] says Costello.

Having to cope with bigotry and hatred can also harm children's mental and physical health. "Experiencing stressful events earlier on in the life course—school age—has significant and lasting effects on health and well-being over a child's life span,"[58] says Sirry Alang, a sociologist at Lehigh University in Bethlehem, Pennsylvania. The stress caused by discrimination (either perceived or real) has been linked to anxiety, depression, obesity, and substance abuse, among other problems. It can affect children's ability to concentrate and to learn. It can also harm their self-esteem, so they start feeling bad about themselves. This may prevent children from speaking up in class or from taking part in activities they once found enjoyable.

Sarah Gerwig-Moore, a law professor at Mercer University in Macon, Georgia, has seen firsthand how painful religious bigotry can be for a child. Gerwig-Moore is a Christian, but her former husband is Jewish, so her two sons identify as members of both faiths. In 2017 she had to console her sixth grader when his best friend drew an art project that featured a swastika. As her son told her what happened, he fought back tears. "His friend was old enough to know what it meant—how it was hurtful—the horrors it had stood for," says Gerwig-Moore. She says her son was hurt and angry, and he felt betrayed by his friend. "There is nothing so heartbreaking as trying to comfort one's child through the pain of senseless rejection," she says. "And once you've felt vicariously the religious discrimination aimed at your own child, such discrimination becomes intolerable from *anyone, anywhere.*"[59]

One Muslim teen who was deeply hurt by what she believed was religious bigotry is Bayan Zehlif from Rancho Cucamonga, California. In May 2016 she saw her photo in the high school yearbook and became distraught over the name that appeared beneath it. Zehlif, who was a junior at the time, was pictured wearing her hijab and smiling, but her name was shown as "Isis Phillips." This was terribly upsetting to Zehlif, and she cried when she first saw it. She then wrote on Facebook, "I am extremely saddened, disgusted, hurt and embarrassed that the Los Osos High School yearbook was able to get away with this. Apparently, I am 'Isis' in the yearbook."[60] The school apologized profusely for the incorrect name, saying it was a terrible mistake. But because Zehlif had experienced anti-Muslim bigotry at school, she was convinced it was a deliberate sign of someone's hatred for her because of her religion. And she found that very hurtful. "Seeing my schoolmates hate me hurts a lot,"[61] she says.

> "Once you've felt vicariously the religious discrimination aimed at your own child, such discrimination becomes intolerable from *anyone, anywhere.*"[59]
>
> —Sarah Gerwig-Moore, a law professor at Mercer University in Macon, Georgia

Wondering Why

Those who are subjected to religious discrimination often do not see it coming, which adds to their confusion as they try to figure out why they were targeted. University of Connecticut student Nathan Schachter, who is Jewish, was shocked in September 2017 by an incident that occurred at school. Everywhere he goes, Schachter wears a *kippah* embroidered with "UConn" in honor of his school. One evening he was walking with some friends when

Traumatized by Bullying

When young people are bullied for any reason, including their religious faith, the experience can be traumatic. It can hurt them emotionally and lead to physical ailments such as stomachaches, headaches, and depression. This was true of an eleven-year-old Muslim boy from Phoenix, Arizona, who was relentlessly bullied during the 2015–2016 school year—by his teacher. According to reports, Faye Myles purposely singled out A.A. (not his real name) because of her personal bigotry toward Muslims. When A.A. asked to pray during recess, she told him no, that praying was not permitted in school. After showing a film about the 9/11 terrorist attacks, she reportedly said to A.A., "That's going to be you," as though he were destined to become a terrorist. A.A. also heard her say, "Muslims shouldn't be given visas. They'll probably take away your visa and deport you." The same day those remarks were made, A.A. was taunted by his classmates, who echoed Myles's disparaging remarks on the school bus, calling him a terrorist, and saying he was going to blow up the bus.

As a result of this treatment, A.A. became upset, anxious, and depressed. He begged his mother not to make him go to school anymore. In October 2016 the American Civil Liberties Union filed a complaint with the DOJ's Civil Rights Division on A.A.'s behalf, requesting that the school and Myles be investigated for violations of federal law.

Quoted in American Civil Liberties Union, "Complaint and Request for Investigation Pursuant to Title IV (letter)," October 28, 2016. www.aclu.org.

a car drove by with several young women in it. Suddenly a back window opened and one of the women yelled out, "Go to the f---ing ovens!"[62] and then drove away. Schachter was stunned, and it took him a few minutes to process what had happened. It finally sank in that because of his religious faith, he had been the target of an anti-Semitic slur, and it troubled him deeply.

Earlier in 2017, a high school freshman from Provo, Utah, was very upset by an incident that occurred on a school bus. Janna Bakeer, who is Muslim and wears a hijab, boarded the bus to ride home from school. The bus driver, speaking over the intercom system, said flippantly, "Hey you with the blue hair thingie, get off the bus, you don't belong here."[63] Bakeer was terribly embarrassed

A Jewish student, who wears a *kippah* on his head, studies outside on a nice day. A Connecticut college student who also wears a *kippah* was shocked to be the target of an anti-Semitic attack.

and hurt by the meanness in the bus driver's tone. She quietly got out of her seat, got off the bus, and called her parents.

School officials later said Bakeer was on the wrong bus, but her parents say that is not the real issue, which is the appalling way she was treated by the driver. "She was mortified," says Randall Spencer, the family's attorney. "She got up and off the bus and was left in the cold parking lot for an hour and a half until her parents could make arrangements to get her." Spencer says that even if she had boarded the wrong bus, embarrassing her because of her hijab was inexcusable. "I don't believe that a young girl [who] was not wearing a hijab would have been treated the same way,"[64] he says.

The Harmful Effects of Bullying

As the prevalence of religious discrimination has steadily risen, incidents of bullying have also risen. Research has shown a surge of bullying cases in schools throughout the United States. According to the 2017 ISPU survey, among people with children in kindergarten through twelfth grade, 42 percent of Muslims, 23 percent of Jews, 20 percent of Protestants, and 6 percent of Catholics report that their children have been bullied because of their religious faith.

A Sikh teen from Utah was relentlessly bullied by his classmates for years. Like all males of the Sikh faith, he did not cut his hair and he wore a smaller version of the turban worn by Sikh men. The boy's appearance became a source of ridicule for children who attended school with him, and this caused him a great deal of hurt and embarrassment. "It started as early as grade one or two," says the teen's mother. "His classmates would tease him about his turban and his long hair, calling him a girl and saying he shouldn't go to the boy's bathroom, or threatening to cut off his

Penalized for Wearing a Hijab

Je'Nan Hayes from Gaithersburg, Maryland, plays basketball on her high school varsity team. Because Hayes is a Muslim, she wears a hijab with her uniform. During her first year of play, the 2016–2017 school year, she was not a starter on the team but played in all twenty-four regular season games. She looked forward to playing in the regional finals, but during the first of those games she was left sitting on the bench. She kept wondering why her coach, Donita Adams, had not called her out onto the court, but she cheered on her team anyway. When the game ended, Adams told her she had been kept out of the game for wearing a hijab.

Just before the game was to start, Adams was approached by the head official and told about a rule forbidding players from wearing any sort of head covering. The rule, which required documented evidence of a religious basis for a player to wear a head covering, was rarely enforced. Still, the official told Adams, Hayes needed to abide by it. When she learned what had happened, she broke down in tears. "I felt discriminated against, and I didn't feel good at all," she says. "If it was some reason like my shirt wasn't the right color or whatever, then I'd be like, 'Okay.' But because of my religion it took it to a whole different level, and I just felt that it was not right at all."

Quoted in Jesse Dougherty, "After Playing All Season, Maryland Girl Held Out of Basketball Game for Wearing a Hijab," *Washington Post*, March 13, 2017. www.washingtonpost.com.

hair in crafts class."[65] Even changing schools did not help. The boy attended a private elementary school, then a public school, but the bullying continued. Finally, the family moved to a different state and settled in a community with a large Sikh population.

One of the biggest and most tragic risks for young people who are bullied is suicide. Research has shown that young people who endure relentless bullying have a high risk of taking their own lives in order to escape from what they perceive as an unbearable situation. Because Muslim children are bullied far more often than children of other religious faiths, their risk of suicide is even higher than others. Farha Abbasi, an assistant professor of psychiatry at Michigan State University and the managing editor of the *Journal of Muslim Mental Health*, says to "think of trauma and toxic stress as putting brick over brick on someone's shoulder. Right now, many Muslim children are carrying a very heavy burden and one more brick can be the breaking point."[66]

Hate Hurts and Harms

Religious discrimination is ugly, hurtful, and sometimes dangerous. In a July 2016 report, Vanita Gupta, the former head of the DOJ's Civil Rights Division, stated, "Communities around the country today—of various faiths, beliefs, and backgrounds—share a series of common concerns. Many feel threatened or discriminated against because of who they are, what they believe, or where they worship."[67] This causes a great deal of pain and suffering for those who are targeted for discrimination, leaving them confused, hurt, embarrassed, and frightened. For young people, who are increasingly affected by religious discrimination, the emotional pain is even harder to bear. No one knows whether the problem will get better in the coming years or if it will grow worse. Civil rights advocates hope for the former, but, unfortunately, fear the latter.

CHAPTER 5

When Religious Beliefs Clash with Civil Rights

Numerous issues related to religious discrimination have garnered media attention, but one in particular has been highly publicized: whether a person's constitutional right to freedom of religion allows him or her to refuse service to certain individuals or groups for religious reasons. There are two distinct viewpoints on this issue—yes and no—and rarely does anyone see the merit of both sides. "The struggle between activists for gay rights and religious freedom has been presented as a zero-sum game where no compromise is possible," says Thomas Reese, a Catholic priest from Washington, DC. "In this contest, gay rights have been presented as the human rights of a persecuted minority which cannot be compromised, while religious freedom has been described as a protection for believers against infringements on their consciences and beliefs."[68] In most cases, one or more of the parties involved believe they are the victims of religious discrimination.

Fighting for First Amendment Rights

One of the court cases in which discrimination versus religious liberty is hotly debated is *Baker v. Hands On Originals*. A promotional printing business in Lexington, Kentucky, Hands On Originals was founded by Blaine Adamson. Over the years it has grown into a successful company that custom designs and prints apparel and accessories for a variety

Citing his religious beliefs, the owner of a Kentucky promotional printing business refused a request to print T-shirts for a gay pride parade. Members of the gay and lesbian organization that ordered the shirts organized a boycott (pictured) and sued.

of customers, particularly Christian organizations, schools, and camps. In 2012 Adamson was asked by the Gay and Lesbian Services Organization (GLSO) to print 504 T-shirts for the local gay pride festival. He politely declined and referred the GLSO to a printer who would be able to meet their needs. Adamson is a devout Christian who believes marriage is between one man and one woman, and he felt that the message he was asked to print on the T-shirts violated his religious beliefs. "I work with and serve gay people," says Adamson. "But I can't print any message that goes against my faith, no matter who asks me to print it."[69]

In March 2012 the GLSO of Lexington filed a discrimination complaint against Hands On Originals with the city's Human Rights Commission, and the commission initially ruled against Adamson's company.

> "I work with and serve gay people. But I can't print any message that goes against my faith, no matter who asks me to print it."[69]
>
> —Blaine Adamson, the owner of a promotional printing business in Lexington, Kentucky

That decision was reversed by a circuit court judge in 2015. As of June 2018, the case had gone through several court decisions and appeals and was before the Kentucky Supreme Court, waiting for a ruling.

Religious Freedom Versus Religious Discrimination

The Hands On Originals case is a prime example of how someone's constitutional right to freely exercise his or her religious beliefs can clash with someone else's right to be free from discrimination. In the viewpoint of Adamson and other like-minded individuals, if the government forces them to provide services, create specialty products, or participate in other endeavors that violate their religious beliefs, this is clearly a form of religious discrimination. Civil rights organizations such as the American Civil Liberties Union (ACLU) and the GLSO disagree, convinced the term *religious freedom* is being used as an excuse to discriminate against people based on their sexual orientation. The ACLU writes that "religious freedom in America means that we all have a right to our religious beliefs, but this does not give us the right to use our religion to discriminate against and impose those beliefs on others who do not share them."[70]

> "Religious freedom in America . . . does not give us the right to use our religion to discriminate against and impose those beliefs on others who do not share them."[70]
>
> —American Civil Liberties Union, which defends people's liberties in accordance with the US Constitution

University of Virginia law professor Doug Laycock disagrees with that sort of argument. He is convinced that Adamson had every right to decline the request for printing gay pride T-shirts in the same way that other printing businesses refuse projects for a variety of different reasons. According to Laycock,

> Just as a pro-choice printer has a right to decline to print a religious message attacking Planned Parenthood, and a gay photographer has a right to decline to photograph a

religious anti-gay rally, a Christian printer who believes in traditional marriage has a right to decline to print materials contradicting that view. The law protects the freedom of individuals in a pluralistic society [one in which people have different beliefs] to disagree.[71]

Support from the Top

The Trump administration has expressed its support for businesses like Adamson's that feel torn between wanting to serve customers fairly while still remaining true to their religious beliefs and conscience. On May 4, 2017, Trump signed an executive order titled "Promoting Free Speech and Religious Liberty." The order covered a number of points, with the gist of it directing the federal government "to vigorously enforce Federal law's robust protections for religious freedom."[72]

The following October, US attorney general Jeff Sessions released a memo that offered more specific guidance for religious liberty protections in federal law. The memo made the federal government's position on protecting religious liberty very clear:

Religious liberty is not merely a right to personal religious beliefs or even to worship in a sacred place. It also encompasses religious observance and practice. Except in the narrowest circumstances, no one should be forced to choose between living out his or her faith and complying with the law. Therefore, to the greatest extent practicable and permitted by law, religious observance and practice should be reasonably accommodated in all government activity, including employment, contracting, and programming.[73]

When the Sessions memo was released, civil rights advocates and groups denounced what they perceived as sanctioned discrimination; in other words, justifying the ability to discriminate against certain individuals under the guise of religious beliefs.

A Transgender Woman's Court Victory

Religion cannot be used as an excuse to discriminate in the workplace. That was the finding in a case involving a transgender woman and her employer, Harris Funeral Homes in Garden City, Michigan. In July 2013 employee Aimee Stephens wrote a letter to owner Thomas Rost. For the six years she had worked for him, she presented as a man and used her then-legal name, William Stephens. In her letter she explained that she had struggled with gender identity disorder her entire life and had decided to transition into a female. She also said she would begin dressing in appropriate women's business attire. Two weeks later Rost fired Stephens. Rost is a devout Christian who considers the funeral home his ministry. He believes that someone's gender is a gift from God and that permitting Stephens to continue working there as a female would violate his religious beliefs.

Stephens filed a complaint with the EEOC, who sued on her behalf in 2014. At the trial, the judge ruled in favor of Harris Funeral Homes, saying the owner had shown that keeping Stephens on staff would impose a substantial burden on his ability to conduct business in accordance with his religious beliefs. A federal appeals court overturned that decision in 2018, ruling in Stephens's favor. ACLU attorney John Knight hailed the decision, saying it "ensures that employers will not be able to use their religious beliefs against trans employees" and there is "no right to discriminate in the workplace."

Quoted in Julie Moreau, "Religion Can't Be Used to Justify Workplace Discrimination, Court Rules," NBC News, March 8, 2018. www.nbcnews.com.

This, opponents warned, could potentially roll back years of civil rights progress. "This administration has taken a very expansive view of religious liberty," says Louise Melling, the ACLU's deputy legal director. "It understands religious liberty to override antidiscrimination principles."[74]

One of the most vocal objectors to the Sessions memo was Dennis J. Herrera, the city attorney for San Francisco. In a statement issued October 6, 2017, the same day as the Sessions memo, Herrera denounced the attorney general's action. "The Sessions-led Justice Department has shown, once again, that it wishes to deny civil rights protections rather than enforce them,"

Herrera wrote. "The attorney general's memo claiming that religious freedom is a license to discriminate is breathtaking in its scope." Herrera went on to say that religious freedom does not give anyone a "license to discriminate," and to pretend otherwise is un-American. "I denounce this attack by the U.S. attorney general on the civil rights of vulnerable individuals and communities,"[75] says Herrera.

Americans Are Divided

With the massive amount of publicity related to religious liberty and discrimination, people throughout the United States often have strong opinions on both sides of the issue. In 2017 the Public Religion Research Institute surveyed more than two thousand people on issues related to religious liberty. When asked if small-business owners should be allowed to refuse to provide products or services to gay individuals if doing so violates their religious beliefs, 64 percent said no, such refusal should not be allowed. Of those, 40 percent strongly opposed such refusals, even for religious reasons.

Other research has shown that many Americans are torn about the religious liberty versus discrimination issue. A December 2017 survey by *Economist* magazine and the market research and data analytics firm YouGov focused on a high-profile case called *Masterpiece Cakeshop v. Colorado Civil Rights Commission*. The case involved a devout Christian baker, Jack Phillips, who creates custom-designed wedding cakes. He declined to make one of his custom creations for a gay couple's wedding reception because same-sex marriage violates his religious beliefs. During the *Economist/YouGov* survey, respondents were asked if they considered it discrimination for a baker to refuse to sell a wedding cake to a same-sex couple if it violates his religious beliefs. Of fifteen hundred participants, 40 percent thought it was discrimination, 40 percent did not think it was discrimination, and the remaining 20 percent were not sure.

The *Masterpiece Cakeshop* Case

Phillips owns Masterpiece Cakeshop in Lakewood, Colorado. In July 2012 Charlie Craig and David Mullins, a gay couple who were planning to get married, visited Phillips's shop and said they would like him to create one of his custom cakes for their wedding reception. Phillips told the men that he could not create their wedding cake because of his religious beliefs. "What a cake celebrating this event would communicate was a message that contradicts my deepest religious convictions," Phillips said in December 2017, "and as an artist, that's just not something I'm able to do, so I politely declined."[76] Phillips offered to sell the couple any cake that was already made and on display in his shop, but he said he could not create a specialty cake for them.

Craig and Mullins, represented by attorneys from the ACLU, filed discrimination charges with the Colorado Civil Rights Commission against Masterpiece Cakeshop. "Religious freedom is undoubtedly an important American value, but so is the right to be treated equally under the law free from discrimination," says

Colorado baker Jack Phillips (pictured) said that baking a custom-made cake for a gay wedding would violate his religious beliefs. The US Supreme Court sided with Phillips but also stressed the importance of maintaining equal rights for gays and lesbians.

Amanda C. Goad, an attorney with the ACLU Lesbian Gay Bisexual and Transgender Project. "Everyone is free to believe what they want, but businesses like Masterpiece Cakeshop cannot treat some customers differently than others based on who they are as people."[77]

After several court decisions and appeals, the US Supreme Court finally agreed to hear the *Masterpiece Cakeshop* case. On June 4, 2018, in a 7–2 ruling, the court sided with Masterpiece Cakeshop. The justices focused on the Colorado Civil Rights Com-

Expanded Protection for Health Care Workers

The Trump administration has often expressed support for medical professionals who object to certain types of medical procedures, such as abortion and gender reassignment surgery. These professionals, including doctors, nurses, and other health care workers, feel that being forced by law to take part in these procedures violates their religious beliefs. So they welcomed a January 2018 announcement by the Trump administration that religious freedom protections for health care workers were being expanded. No longer would they be required by law to participate in medical procedures that violated their conscience. This expanded protection for health care workers is overseen by a new division of the US Department of Health and Human Services called the Conscience and Religious Freedom division.

A few weeks after the announcement, a pediatric nurse from Rockford, Illinois, filed a claim against her former employer. Sandra Rojas had been a pediatric nurse with the county health department for eighteen years. She objected to a policy enacted in 2015 that required nurses to be trained to make referrals to abortion providers and to help women obtain abortion drugs. When she informed her employer of her conscientious objection to having any involvement in abortions, she was forced to resign from her job. Speaking of her frustration with longstanding government policy, Rojas writes: "Unfortunately, the government has failed both health care professionals and the patients they serve. Rather than fulfilling its legal obligation to protect conscience, it has instead sought to coerce health care professionals to violate their conscience and participate in procedures that end life."

Diane Black and Sandra Rojas, "Protecting Nurses' Conscience: A Non-Negotiable in the Final FY 2018 Spending Bill," *Hill*, March 9, 2018. http://thehill.com.

mission, the board that originally heard the case, because they found its treatment of Phillips to be troubling. The commission's basic premise was that regardless of his beliefs, Phillips must either bake cakes for gay weddings or get out of the cake business. According to the Supreme Court, the commission demonstrated such open hostility toward Phillips's religious beliefs that it violated his First Amendment rights. "The Commission's treatment of Phillips' case violated the State's duty under the First Amendment not to base laws or regulations on hostility to a religion or religious viewpoint," Justice Anthony Kennedy wrote. He continued: "The neutral and respectful consideration to which Phillips was entitled was compromised here. The Civil Rights Commission's treatment of his case has some elements of a clear and impermissible hostility toward the sincere religious beliefs that motivated his objection."[78]

The Supreme Court's narrow ruling left open the question of whether other bakers, photographers, or florists could be cited for discrimination should they decline to provide services for a same-sex wedding. The issue seems destined for the Supreme Court once again in the near future.

The Bridal Boutique Case

Another highly publicized case involving the clash between religious freedom and civil rights began in July 2017 at a Bloomsburg, Pennsylvania, bridal shop called WW Bridal Boutique. A lesbian couple, Shannon Kennedy and Julie Ann Samanas, visited the boutique to look at wedding dresses for their March 2018 wedding. They filled out a form and listed Samanas's name under *Bride*. Then they crossed out the word *Groom*, replaced it with *Bride*, and wrote Kennedy's name in the space. They handed the form to one of two women working at the boutique who asked them if the dress they wanted was for a same-sex wedding. Upon learning that it was, the employee said. "I don't know if you've heard, but we're Christian and we don't believe in that; our faith doesn't let us believe in that."[79]

Feeling stunned, Kennedy and Samanas left the shop without incident. They wrote about what happened on social media, and word spread fast. A woman named Jenn Shepard, who had a similar experience with a florist when she was planning her wedding, started a Facebook group called Boycott WW Bridal Boutique in which she urged customers not to patronize the shop. "The bottom line is this: When you have a public business centered around serving the public, that's what you do—you serve the public, the ENTIRE public," Shepard wrote. "Not just the ones you prefer or approve of. As an individual, one can worship and practice any of the gods or religions they wish, that is a personal right and freedom for all Americans. But when you are a business owner who serves the public, your personal beliefs must not interfere with your ability to serve the public equally."[80]

Largely because of how far and wide word spread on social media, Victoria Miller, the owner of the bridal boutique, began receiving vulgar e-mails, hate mail, and death threats. One person threatened to shoot her in the head, and another threatened to burn the boutique down. In an e-mail to one media source, Miller explained, "We have provided formalwear for our customers from all walks of life, including the LGBTQ community. We have always served everyone with respect and dignity. It is just this event, a same-sex marriage, which we cannot participate in due to our personal convictions."[81] Refusing to back down, which she believed would violate her religious beliefs, Miller closed WW Bridal Boutique on March 30, 2018, after thirty-seven years in business.

The Flower Shop Case

Barronelle Stutzman is another business owner who found herself at the center of a legal dispute because of a decision she made based on her Christian beliefs. Stutzman's flower shop, Arlene's Flowers, is located in Richland, Washington. For years she had been friends with a gay man named Rob Ingersoll. "Rob and I hit it off from the beginning because, like me, he looks at flowers

The owner of Arlene's Flowers in Washington cited religious beliefs for her decision to turn down a request to design floral arrangements for a same-sex wedding. The state Supreme Court ruled against the floral shop owner, but the case is still pending.

GRAB AND GO
BOUQUETS
9.95

with an artist's eye," says Stutzman. She knew that Ingersoll was in a relationship with another man, and he knew that she was a Christian. But that did not affect their friendship—until he asked her to design floral arrangements for his wedding, and she turned him down. Because of her Christian faith, Stutzman believes that marriage is only between a man and a woman. Thus, she said, she could not create floral arrangements for Ingersoll's wedding. "It was a painful thing to try to explain to someone I cared about— one of the hardest things I've ever done in my life," she says.

"But Rob assured me he understood. . . . We seemed to part as friends. But then I was sued."[82]

A lower court ruled against Stutzman, and an appeals court affirmed that ruling. The case was heard by the Washington Supreme Court in 2017, and in February of that year the justices also ruled against Stutzman. Late in 2017 attorneys from the Alliance Defending Freedom asked the US Supreme Court to hear Stutzman's case. As of June 18, 2018, the justices were still considering the attorneys' request.

A Complicated, Contentious Issue

The right for people to practice the religion of their choosing is well established in the United States, thanks to the US Constitution's First Amendment. Also well established is the right to be free from discrimination based on race, religion, gender, or sexual orientation. But when those two fundamental principles of American society clash with each other, this can cause serious problems for all parties involved. The Trump administration has shown its support for business owners and others who feel they are being discriminated against when they must choose between serving the public and remaining true to their religious convictions. On the other hand, the ACLU and other civil rights groups believe religion is being used as an excuse to discriminate against people who do not share their religious views. Those who are able to see both sides of the issue view it as a problem with no easy solution. In the words of attorney Peter Kirsanow, who is a member of the US Commission on Civil Rights, "The conflict between religious liberty and nondiscrimination principles is profound."[83]

> "The conflict between religious liberty and nondiscrimination principles is profound."[83]
>
> —Peter Kirsanow, an attorney and a member of the US Commission on Civil Rights

SOURCE NOTES

Introduction: The Ugliness of Bigotry

1. Quoted in Justin Glawe, "Alleged Texas Mosque Arsonist Thought Mosque Was ISIS, Feds Say," Daily Beast, March 10, 2017. www.thedailybeast.com.
2. Quoted in Fauzeya Rahman, "Community Works to Rebuild Following Devastating Mosque Blaze," San Antonio Express-News, February 2, 2017. www.expressnews.com.
3. Linda K. Wertheimer, "How Schools Overlook Religious Harassment and What to Do About It," Washington Post, January 8, 2016. www.washingtonpost.com.
4. Vanita Gupta, "Combating Religious Discrimination Today: Final Report," US Department of Justice, July 2016. www.justice.gov.

Chapter 1: How Serious a Problem Is Religious Discrimination?

5. Legal Information Institute, "U.S. Constitution: First Amendment," Cornell Law School. www.law.cornell.edu.
6. Quoted in Kyra Gurney, "Florida Teachers Called Their Middle Eastern Students 'Terrorists' and It Cost Them," Miami Herald, August 11, 2017. www.miamiherald.com.
7. Quoted in CBS News, "Muslim Officer Claims 'Blatant Racism and Bigotry' Within SFPD," April 10, 2018. http://sanfrancisco.cbslocal.com.
8. Anti-Defamation League, "Audit of Anti-Semitic Incidents: Year in Review, 2017," February 2018. www.adl.org.
9. Quoted in Leslie Postal, "After Swastika Found on Seminole School Bus, Mom Wants Incident Discussed," Orlando Sentinel, February 28, 2017. www.orlandosentinel.com.
10. Quoted in Joyce Tsai, "Anti-Semitism on the Island," Alameda Magazine, September 27, 2017. www.alamedamagazine.com.

11. Quoted in Sarah Parvini, "Being Sikh in Trump's America: 'You Have to Go Out of Your Way to Prove You're Not a Threat,'" *Los Angeles Times*, June 11, 2017. www.latimes.com.

12. Quoted in Homeland Security Digital Library, "Responses to the Increase in Religious Hate Crimes," Naval Postgraduate School, Center for Homeland Defense and Security, May 2, 2017. www.hsdl.org.

13. Lisa Guerin, "Workplace Harassment Based on Religion," Nolo. www.nolo.com.

14. US Department of Justice, "Combating Religious Discrimination and Protecting Religious Freedom," December 4, 2017. www.justice.gov.

15. Quoted in Sam Levin, "Muslim Women Kicked Out of California Restaurant Sue for Discrimination," *Guardian*, May 4, 2016. www.theguardian.com.

16. Quoted in US Department of Education, "US Department of Education Takes Actions to Address Religious Discrimination," news release, July 22, 2016. www.ed.gov.

17. US Department of Justice, "Combating Religious Discrimination and Protecting Religious Freedom."

Chapter 2: Religious Hate Crimes

18. James B. Comey, "The FBI and the ADL: Working Toward a World Without Hate," FBI News, April 28, 2014. www.fbi.gov.

19. Quoted in Erika Norton, "Warwick Teen Arrested in Jewish Cemetery Vandalism Case," *Warwick Advertiser*, November 2, 2017. www.warwickadvertiser.com.

20. Quoted in Evan Wilt, "Religious Hate Crimes Are on the Rise." *World*, May 2, 2017. https://world.wng.org.

21. Quoted in Larry Celona, "'I Will Cut Your Throat!': Man Attacks Muslim Cop and Her Son," *New York Post*, December 5, 2016. https://nypost.com.

22. Brian Levin, "Jews Top Target for Hate Crimes Last Year in New York City, Again," *Huffington Post*, January 10, 2018. www.huffingtonpost.com.

23. Quoted in Ken Schwencke, "Why America Fails at Gathering Hate Crime Statistics," ProPublica, December 4, 2017. www.propublica.org.

24. Quoted in Anti-Defamation League, "ADL Calls for Action After New FBI Data Shows Rise in Hate Crimes," November 13, 2017. www.adl.org.

25. Quoted in Ken Schwencke and A.C. Thompson, "More than 100 Federal Law Enforcement Agencies Fail to Report Hate Crimes to the FBI," *Mother Jones*, June 27, 2017. www.motherjones.com.

26. Schwencke, "Why America Fails at Gathering Hate Crime Statistics."

27. Quoted in Schwencke, "Why America Fails at Gathering Hate Crime Statistics."

28. Quoted in Laura Santhanam and Kenya Downs, "Why Hate Crimes Are So Difficult to Convict," *PBS NewsHour*, January 6, 2017. www.pbs.org.

29. Rachel Glickhouse, "What We Discovered During a Year of Documenting Hate," ProPublica, December 26, 2017. www.propublica.org.

30. Quoted in Wilt, "Religious Hate Crimes Are on the Rise."

31. Quoted in Homeland Security Digital Library, "Responses to the Increase in Religious Hate Crimes."

32. Quoted in Maya Salam, "Two Men Are Sentenced to 3 Years for Attack on Sikh Man," *New York Times*, May 18, 2017. www.nytimes.com.

33. Federal Bureau of Investigation, "Hate Crimes," 2017. www.fbi.gov.

34. Erwin Chemerinsky, "Hate Speech Is Protected Free Speech, Even on College Campuses," Vox, December 26, 2017. www.vox.com.

35. Liaquat Ali Khan, "Interconnectivity: Hate Crimes Against Jews and Muslims," CounterPunch, February 28, 2018. www.counterpunch.org.

36. Quoted in Mark Berman, "Hate Crimes in the United States Increased Last Year, the FBI Says," *Washington Post*, November 13, 2017. www.washingtonpost.com.

Chapter 3: Religious Discrimination in the Workplace

37. Equal Employment Opportunity Commission, "Questions and Answers: Religious Discrimination in the Workplace," January 31, 2011. www.eeoc.gov.

38. Anti-Defamation League, "Religious Accommodation in the Workplace: Your Rights and Obligations," 2015. www.adl .org.

39. Quoted in Alison Moodie, "Are US Businesses Doing Enough to Support Religious Diversity in the Workplace?," *Guardian*, January 28, 2016. www.theguardian.com.

40. Jason A. Cantone and Richard L. Wiener, "Religion at Work: Evaluating Hostile Work Environment Religious Discrimination Claims," *Psychology Public Policy and Law*, July 2017, pp. 351–66.

41. Cantone and Wiener, "Religion at Work."

42. Quoted in Kate McGovern Tornone, "Religious Discrimination Hazards on the Rise," HR Daily Advisor, March 27, 2017. https://hrdailyadvisor.blr.com.

43. Barbara Hoey and Alyssa Smilowitz, "The Rise of Employee Religious Discrimination Claims," Law 360, October 17, 2017. www.law360.com.

44. Equal Employment Opportunity Commission, "Religious Discrimination." www.eeoc.gov.

45. Quoted in Josefin Dolsten, "Orthodox Jewish Paramedic Sues NY Hospital over Its No-Skirts Policy," Jewish Telegraphic Agency, May 24, 2017. www.jta.org.

46. Quoted in Equal Employment Opportunity Commission, "Abercrombie Resolves Religious Discrimination Case Following Supreme Court Ruling in Favor of EEOC," July 28, 2015. www.eeoc.gov.

47. J. William Manuel, "The Devil Is in the . . . Biometric Scanner? Fourth Circuit Finds Employer Failed to Accommodate Employee's Religious Belief," Labor & Employment Insights, June 14, 2017. www.employmentlawinsights.com.

48. Quoted in Andrew Keshner and James Fanelli, "Workers Win $5.1M Payout for Enduring Ex-Employers' 'Cult-Like' Ideas," *New York Daily News*, April 29, 2018. www.nydaily news.com.

49. Quoted in Equal Employment Opportunity Commission, "Jury Awards $5.1 Million for Workers in EEOC Religious Discrimination Case Against United Health Programs of America, Inc. and Cost Containment Group, Inc.," April 26, 2018. www1 .eeoc.gov.

50. Quoted in Erik Avanier and Jenese Harris, "Knife, Stun Gun Pulled in Dispute at St. Augustine McDonald's," News4JAX, May 23, 2018. www.news4jax.com.

51. Quoted in Meagan Flynn, "'You Don't Deserve American Food!': Muslim Students Attacked at McDonald's, Police Say," *Washington Post*, May 25, 2018. www.washingtonpost.com.

52. Quoted in Jenna Johnson, "Trump Calls for 'Total and Complete Shutdown of Muslims Entering the United States,'" *Washington Post*, December 7, 2015. www.washingtonpost .com.

53. Quoted in Anna North, "When Hate Leads to Depression," *New York Times*, April 17, 2017. www.nytimes.com.

54. Quoted in Jenée Desmond-Harris, "'Crying Is an Everyday Thing': Life After Trump's 'Muslim Ban' at a Majority-Immigrant School," Vox, February 16, 2017. www.vox.com.

55. Maureen B. Costello, "The Trump Effect," Southern Poverty Law Center, November 28, 2016. www.splcenter.org.

56. Quoted in Antonia Blumberg, "The US Has Started Tracking Religious Discrimination in Schools," *Huffington Post*, September 12, 2016. www.huffingtonpost.com.

57. Costello, "The Trump Effect."

58. Quoted in Desmond-Harris, "'Crying Is an Everyday Thing.'"

59. Sarah Gerwig-Moore, "Reaping the Whirlwind: Reflections on Passover, Easter, and a New Age of Religious Discrimination," *Telegraph*, April 14, 2017. www.macon.com.

60. Quoted in Doug Saunders, "Muslim Student Misidentified as 'Isis' in Los Osos High Yearbook," *Daily Bulletin*, May 8, 2016. www.dailybulletin.com.

61. Quoted in Dean Obeidallah, "Anti-Muslim School Bullying: Sometimes, It's Even the Teachers Doing It," Daily Beast, May 18, 2016. www.thedailybeast.com.

62. Quoted in Marlese Lessing, "UConn Student 'Shocked' by Anti-Semitic Comment," *Daily Campus*, September 8, 2017. http://dailycampus.com.

63. Quoted in Kurt Hanson and Braley Dodson, "Family Asking Provo City School District for Apology After Daughter Wearing

Hijab Singled Out on Bus," *Daily Herald*, January 10, 2017. www.heraldextra.com.

64. Quoted in Hanson and Dodson, "Family Asking Provo City School District for Apology After Daughter Wearing Hijab Singled Out on Bus."

65. Quoted in Kelsey Dallas, "Reading, Writing, and Respect: How to Protect Your Kids from Faith-Based Bullying," *Deseret News*, August 25, 2016. www.deseretnews.com.

66. Quoted in Alison Kodjak, "Teen Bullies and Their Victims Both Face a Higher Risk of Suicide," NPR, June 28, 2016. www.npr.org.

67. Gupta, "Combating Religious Discrimination Today."

Chapter 5: When Religious Beliefs Clash with Civil Rights

68. Thomas Reese, "Time for Compromise on Gay Rights and Religious Freedom," *Faith and Justice* (blog), *National Catholic Reporter*, December 1, 2016. www.ncronline.org.

69. Blaine Adamson, "I'm a T-Shirt Maker with Gay Customers and Gay Employees. I Still Was Sued," *Daily Signal*, September 17, 2017. www.dailysignal.com.

70. American Civil Liberties Union, "Using Religion to Discriminate," 2018. www.aclu.org.

71. Quoted in Becket Fund for Religious Liberty, "Baker v. Hands On Originals," 2018. www.becketlaw.org.

72. Quoted in Emma Green, "Why Trump's Executive Order on Religious Liberty Left Many Conservatives Dissatisfied," *Atlantic*, May 4, 2017. www.theatlantic.com.

73. Jefferson Sessions, "Memorandum for All Executive Departments and Agencies," press release, Office of the Attorney General, US Department of Justice, October 6, 2017. www.justice.gov.

74. Quoted in Alison Kodjak, "Trump Administration Will Shield Health Workers Citing Religion to Refuse Care," NPR, January 18, 2018. www.npr.org.

75. Dennis J. Herrera, "Statement from City Attorney Dennis Herrera on Sessions' 'Religious Liberty' Memo," City Attorney of San Francisco, October 6, 2017. www.sfcityattorney.org.

76. Jack Phillips, "This Is Why I Can't Custom-Make Cakes for Same-Sex Weddings," *USA Today*, December 4, 2017. www .usatoday.com.

77. Quoted in ACLU Colorado, "Colorado Civil Rights Commission Finds Bakery Discriminated Against Gay Couple," May 30, 2014. https://aclu-co.org.

78. Anthony Kennedy, "Masterpiece Cakeshop, Ltd., et al. *v.* Colorado Civil Rights Commission et al.," June 4, 2018. www .supremecourt.gov.

79. Quoted in Jen Colletta, "Lesbian Couple Turned Away from PA Bridal Shop," *Philadelphia Gay News*, July 19, 2017. www .epgn.com.

80. Quoted in Bill Wellock, "Bridal Shop That Refused Couple Will Close," *Citizens Voice*, March 10, 2018. http://citizensvoice .com.

81. Quoted in Curtis M. Wong, "This Bridal Shop Is Under Fire (Again) for Turning Away a Lesbian Couple," *Huffington Post*, July 24, 2017. www.huffingtonpost.com.

82. Barronelle Stutzman, "Why a Friend Is Suing Me: The Arlene's Flowers Story," *Seattle Times*, November 12, 2015. www .seattletimes.com.

83. Quoted in Joe Davidson, "Civil Rights or Religious Liberty— What's on Top?" *Washington Post*, September 9, 2016. www .washingtonpost.com.

ORGANIZATIONS AND WEBSITES

American Civil Liberties Union (ACLU)

125 Broad St., 18th Floor
New York, NY 10004
website: www.aclu.org

The ACLU works with courts, legislatures, and communities to defend and preserve the rights and liberties that are guaranteed for all Americans under the US Constitution. Its website offers a number of articles, reports, and opinion pieces about religious discrimination.

Anti-Defamation League

823 United Nations Plaza
New York, NY 10017
website: www.adl.org

The Anti-Defamation League fights anti-Semitism and all forms of bigotry, defends democratic ideals, and protects civil rights for all. Its website offers a resource library with a wealth of articles and other publications about religious discrimination.

Equal Employment Opportunity Commission (EEOC)

131 M St. NE
Washington, DC 20507
website: www.eeoc.gov

The EEOC is charged with enforcing federal antidiscrimination laws related to every aspect of employment. The website offers a comprehensive collection of materials, with the search engine producing hundreds of articles about religious discrimination and related issues.

Heritage Foundation

214 Massachusetts Ave. NE
Washington, DC 20002-4999
website: www.heritage.org

The Heritage Foundation is a research and education institution that supports conservative public policies based on limited government and individual freedom. Thousands of articles related to religious freedom and religious discrimination are available through the website's search engine.

Public Religion Research Institute (PRRI)

2027 Massachusetts Ave. NW, Floor 3
Washington, DC 20036
website: www.prri.org

The PRRI is a nonprofit, nonpartisan research and education organization that conducts public opinion polls on a variety of different topics, including religious discrimination. Its website features a number of different publications related to religious discrimination.

Southern Poverty Law Center

400 Washington Ave.
Montgomery, AL 36104
website: www.splcenter.org

The Southern Poverty Law Center is dedicated to fighting hate and bigotry and to seeking justice for society's most vulnerable people. Its website's search engine produces articles, reports, and other publications about religious discrimination and related topics.

US Department of Education

400 Maryland Ave. SW
Washington, DC 20202
website: www.ed.gov

An agency of the federal government, the US Department of Education establishes policy for, administers, and coordinates most federal assistance to the US education system. Its website offers a wide variety of publications related to religious discrimination.

Books

John Allen, *Threats to Civil Liberties: Religion*. San Diego: ReferencePoint, 2019.

John Corvino, Ryan T. Anderson, and Sherif Girgis, *Debating Religious Liberty and Discrimination*. New York: Oxford University Press, 2017.

Internet Sources

Daniel Cox and Molly Fisch-Friedman, "As Hate Crimes Rise, Young People Perceive Religious Discrimination of Muslims and Jewish People Differently," Public Religion Research Institute, March 22, 2018. www.prri.org/spotlight/different -perceptions-of-religious-discrimination.

Matt Ford, "Religious Liberty or Discrimination?," *Atlantic*, October 6, 2017. www.theatlantic.com/politics/archive /2017/10/religious-liberty-or-lgbt-discrimination/542325.

Sarah Gerwig-Moore, "Reaping the Whirlwind: Reflections on Passover, Easter, and a New Age of Religious Discrimination," *Telegraph*, April 14, 2017. www.macon.com/opinion /readers-opinion/article144608054.html.

Abigail Hauslohner, "Southern Poverty Law Center Says American Hate Groups Are on the Rise," *Washington Post*, February 15, 2017. www.washingtonpost.com/national /southern-poverty-law-center-says-american-hate-groups -are-on-the-rise/2017/02/15/7e9cab02-f2d9-11e6-a9b0 -ecee7ce475fc_story.html?utm_term=.5e9c92e273cd.

Jenna Johnson, "Trump Calls for 'Total and Complete Shutdown of Muslims Entering the United States,'" *Washington Post*, December 7, 2015. www.washingtonpost.com/news /post-politics/wp/2015/12/07/donald-trump-calls-for-total -and-complete-shutdown-of-muslims-entering-the-united -states/?utm_term=.c095ae13f19a.

Sarah Parvini, "Being Sikh in Trump's America: 'You Have to Go Out of Your Way to Prove You're Not a Threat,'" *Los Angeles Times*, June 11, 2017. www.latimes.com/local/california/la-me -trump-sikhs-20170509-htmlstory.html.

Emily Wagster Pettus, "Lawsuit: Waitress Fired over Religious Objection to Pants," *Chicago Tribune*, September 26, 2017. www.chicagotribune.com/sns-bc-us--blue-jeans-discrimination -lawsuit-20170926-story.html.

Cam Smith, "Maryland Basketball Player Held out of Final Game for Wearing Hijab," *Outside the Box* (blog), *USA Today*, March 14, 2017. http://usatodayhss.com/2017/maryland-basketball -player-held-out-of-final-game-for-wearing-hijab.

INDEX